No Cl

By the same author

Bottled Up: How to survive living with a problem drinker
(Lion Books)

First Steps out of Problem Drinking [First Steps series]
(Lion Books)

No Cloistered Life

John McMahon

First published in 2026 by Highland Books, 1 Fairfield Close, Exmouth, EX8 2BN

Copyright © 2026 John McMahon. The moral right of John McMahon as author has been asserted.

All rights reserved. No part of this publication may be reproduced, stored or transmitted in any form or by any means, electronic, mechanical, photocopying, recording, scanning, or otherwise without written permission from the publisher. It is illegal to copy this book, post it to a website, or distribute it by any other means without permission.

ISBN-13: 978-1-897913-99-4

ISBN-10: 1-897913-99-0

Ebook ISBN: 978-1-909690-99-8

Printed in the UK by CPI Books

Contents

	Introduction	7
1:	Of Google and a Message from the Top	11
2:	My Family	19
3:	Are Your Pants Clean?	39
4:	Understanding God	51
5:	Back to School	64
6:	First Job	72
7:	Mary Rose	76
8:	Drop Out	82
9:	Jesus Loves	95
10:	Sandra	107
11:	Alcohol	122
12:	Came to Believe	133
13:	Fiona	138
14:	Academia	159
15:	Sheila	174
16:	If Conclusion Jumping was an Olympic Sport	187
17:	An Appointment with God	195
18:	Commissioning	207
19:	Leaving Scotland	218
20:	You Believe What?	233
	Epilogue	253

Dedication

I have been blessed by the love and companionship of some remarkable women. This book is for them. Thank you to all of them, especially to Lou.

And of course, thank you to God for his patience and faithfulness.

Introduction

Where do you start a book like this? I suppose I could start at the beginning, when I was born. Or I could start it when I first went to school and learned that Catholics and Protestants were two different species. Or I could start it in my childhood, when I became an altar boy. Or I could start it in my early teens, when I entered the seminary to train to be a priest. Or I could start it in my early 20s when I was a hippy and joined a Christian commune. Or I could start it in my 30s, when I was a hopeless alcoholic in a psychiatric ward, and got sober through AA. Or I could start it in my 40s, when I was awarded my doctorate in psychology. Or I could start it in my 50s, when, like the prodigal son, I returned to God. Any of these points would be a viable point to begin this book. However, I feel my starting point needs to be a specific date (2nd April 2012).

Clearly, my story did not start that day, but the idea for this book did. I was out having a walk and had stopped on a bench near the university in Exeter. It was a beautiful spring day, with the sun streaming through the trees. Just the sort of day that was perfect to sit on the bench to pray and meditate; a fairly recent habit I was trying to develop. My fledgling business wasn't exactly booming, so I wanted to pray about it and search for guidance about a way forward.

Instead of getting the hoped-for answers to my business questions, I heard God say, "I want you to write a book about your life as an ordinary saint."

"Sorry, you want me to do what? Who wants to hear about me and, besides, I'm no saint. OK, sometimes I think I am, especially when I'm arguing with my wife. I mean, a saint is a holy man and come on; nobody who knows me is going to seriously suggest that I fit that description."

"Many people will be interested in hearing about you. But the book is not about you alone. It is your relationship with me, that is the core of the book. And a saint is not a 'holy man' as you call it, that is a very human definition. I see it in a different light, my definition of a saint is someone I have chosen, and I have chosen you."

"OK, that's nice, thanks, but why an ordinary saint?"

"All the saints were ordinary. It was their relationship with me that made them extraordinary. I want people to see that if you, with all your scepticism, doubts and misgivings can come to have a relationship with me, then anyone can."

"I'm not sure that was a compliment."

"Do you need one? Well, I love you as you are."

"Hmmm"

If you are still reading this book, and you are not a practising Christian, then you might be wondering if you have just picked up a book written by a madman, or maybe a fantasy book. There is an old saying, although I don't remember who said it: if you speak to God, you are devout; if he speaks to you, you are crazy.

In that case, I am crazy as a coot (whatever that is). God does speak to me. Sometimes he speaks very clearly, sometimes less so and sometimes through writings, such as the Bible or daily meditations, and sometimes through other people. Does that make me special? Yes and no – I do believe that God has chosen me, but he has not only he has chosen all of us, you too! He invites us all to enter into a personal relationship with him. So I am not so special to receive the invitation, although to be invited into a relationship with God is pretty special, is it not?!

What really makes us special is what happens if we accept that invitation. That is what this book is about, the transformation, transcendence and struggle that came when I said yes to a relationship with God. It is a love story, a romance, an adventure and a mystery all rolled into one. It is my story, but it is not unique.

The book is not really an autobiography as people would normally understand the term. Although it does contain lots of events from my life, some of them even in chronological order. Think of it more as a photo album, rather than a video. It is a book mostly about my relationship with God and coming to a personal understanding of who he is and how he works. It is a very personal book, full of personal insights. It is not a theological thesis; I'm not qualified to produce one. But even if I was, that is not the purpose here. My intention in this book is to pour out my personal story, my thoughts, prejudices, struggles, enlightenments and encounters with God (what Christians would call my testimony).

One thread runs through this book, namely that it is a journey. Some people travel huge distances in miles and don't move at all in their hearts; others remain where they are and move enormous distances in their hearts. For me, it is a bit of both, I have done some travelling and, hopefully, I have moved a long way in my heart also. You can be the one to decide.

1: Of Google and a Message from the Top

I blame Google for all of this; the power to search for anyone and anything makes it so tempting. Who hasn't done it? Who hasn't googled their ex-girlfriend, boyfriend, wife, husband, school bully or whoever? C'mon, own up, you have, haven't you? You just type in their name and instantly you have the details of their life, career, even social life, and their last meal, especially if they are avid and embarrassing Facebook users. That sort of power, to be able to spy unseen, is just far too tempting to resist. Well, at least it was for me.

That is how all this started. I had originally met Lou when we were both in our early 20s and we had a relationship for a while, until she dumped me in London that is. And then, almost 35 years later, I googled her to see what I could find out about her. It wasn't easy, she was one of only a dozen people worldwide that was not a Facebook user. In fact, she was not even much of an internet user at all. However, eventually, after many false starts, I found the right Lou, not the doctor who was licensed to practice at boxing matches in the USA, the marine engineer, the American football coach or the assorted other people who shared her name. It is amazing how many people out there, do share a name. Anyway, I found that she was married, had a son and a daughter and lived in Exeter, and I even got an address.

So now you know what has happened to the old flame, you have tracked her down and you know what she has done in her life. But what do you do with the information? Do you just arrive on the doorstep and say "Hi, remember me. I know I have not seen, spoken to, or been in touch with you for 35 years, but it is time to celebrate as here I am now. You must be absolutely over the moon to see me." "What do you mean who am I? And why are you not delighted that the wait is finally over and I have turned up at last?" No, you're right, that does seem a bit crazy, doesn't it. What also made it a bit more difficult was that she lived in Devon on the south coast of England, while I lived on the other side of the country, in Scotland.

So I did the only sensible thing, I decided to just forget that I had found out anything about her and consign the memory to the dead file zone of my brain. This is the zone that contains all the things I have forgotten, the one part of my brain that seems to be getting bigger as I get older. But have you ever tried to forget something like that? Not easy is it? In fact there is actually a name for this phenomenon 'the white bear problem' that states that the more you try to forget something, the more you actually remember it. Well, I had opened up a channel to the past, and it would not close now. But I had made a definite decision, I was not going to do anything about it, absolutely no way – or so I thought. By now you probably surmise that I did not follow my own advice – nothing new there.

A few weeks later I was returning from a holiday in Slovenia, a really beautiful little country. However, Ljubljana airport is not the most interesting or exciting place in the world. Almost the only things to do there are drink coffee and people watch. So while I drank coffee and watched people, I was treated to a parade of Lou-alikes. They were everywhere. Everyone, even the person serving me coffee, seemed to have some characteristic that reminded me of Lou. They somehow reminded me of how she looked then or might look now. Isn't it funny that when we have not seen someone for years, our mind keeps them looking exactly the same, but to account for the passing of time it adds a little bit of grey, a bit like some poor movie makeup. Unfortunately, life seldom ages us quite as sympathetically as our minds do, such a pity.

When I got back home, I again tried to bury the memory, but I had no more success this time than I had had previously. Instead, I decided to take a more proactive approach, after all I'm a psychologist, I know how to deal with these sorts of situations. I would write her a letter and get the obsession out of my system, but obviously I would not post it – no, that would just be far too crazy. This was just going to be a brain dump, a way to get it out of my system, an exercise we psychologists would call a catharsis, absolutely nothing more. No way José!

To cut a long story short, I wrote the letter, walked around with it in my pocket for a few weeks and then eventually I weakened and posted it. When I put the letter in the post box, I had no idea how it would completely transform my life.

I dropped the letter into our village post box with a mixture of emotions. I had no idea what would come from it, I suspected that the most that would happen is that I would get a polite reply and a new name on my

Xmas card list or, at the other extreme – a restraining order. Nothing really prepared me for what actually did happen, but then nothing had prepared Lou either.

I posted the letter on Friday around noon. The next day also around noon the phone rang and the voice said, "Hi this is Lou here".

It took me a while to find my voice, this was not something that I had actually expected, as I said a polite reply at best, but more likely nothing at all. Instead, here I was standing open mouthed, with my past talking to me on the phone.

As you might imagine it was a bit awkward at first, but soon the years and the distance melted away and we were chatting as if we had last met the day before. We filled each other in on our lives since we last met, marriages, children, jobs and all the other events and circumstances that carve our names on the fabric of history. One thing seemed to hang over the conversation; it certainly stirred up a huge welter of emotions in me. Lou announced (maybe announced is too dramatic a word from her viewpoint, from mine it is too small) "I'm a widow!" Why that should have made such an impact was a bit of a mystery. I had no designs on a new relationship (or even dusting off an old one), in fact in the next few months we told each other often, and at great length, how much we were not looking for a relationship. It felt a bit like a competition of who was looking for a relationship the least.

You have probably guessed by now that we started a relationship. In fact we are now married. It was probably the only way to resolve the issue of who wanted a relationship the least. But before we got married there were some highly significant and even practical events which had to happen.

Of course, the first thing was that we had to meet, always a good start. However, it did not happen immediately. We chatted on the phone at fortnightly intervals to begin with, then weekly. Then Lou suggested that I might come down to Exeter sometime, a suggestion that both excited and terrified me in equal measure. After talking this over with some friends, who suggested that I needed to go and just see what happens, I decided to go to Exeter. I have never been a nervous flier. In fact I usually enjoy it, apart from the sheer unremitting boredom of long-haul flights.

However, that flight was quite possibly the most nerve-wracking one that I have ever experienced. I was like a teenage boy on his first date, heart hammering, palms sweating and being eyed very suspiciously by the stewardess in case I was a hijacker or terrorist. Although where I was likely to divert the plane to is anyone's guess "Take me to the Isle of Wight" doesn't have the same ring to it as many, or even any other destinations.

Eventually, after what seemed like a lifetime, the plane arrived. I emerged into the arrivals lounge and there we were face to face for the first time in 35 years. At least I hoped that was her. The last time I had seen her she was 21, gorgeous and had hair to her waist. I was a year older, a hippy complete with beads and tie-dye shirt and hair way down my back. Time could have been kinder to us, for example my long hair was a distant memory, come to think of it, so was most of the rest of my hair. One consolation was that clearly neither of us had run short of food in the interim years. After about half an hour the changes of the years melted away and we were Lou and John again.

The afternoon was spent having lunch, talking, walking, talking, sightseeing, talking and oh yeah, talking. The atmosphere was relaxed and easy, especially after we had assured each other, quite a few times, that we were not looking for a relationship. Yes, we were quite clear about that, it seemed important to state it clearly and often, just in case there was any misunderstanding. The next day we were going to go to Sidmouth, a seaside town near Exeter. This was a real nostalgic trip for both of us. Lou had lived there for much of her early life after her parents had moved from London. And that was where I had met her, when I was a hippy sleeping on the beach. So the visit to Sidmouth was going to be one of the highlights of this trip. Before we set off, Lou said that she needed to talk to me first. Oh I really hate when people do that. It feels like they have found out my dirty little secrets (maybe some that even I don't know) and now I am about to be exposed. In light of what happened nothing could have been closer to, or further away from the truth.

Lou ushered me into the kitchen and we sat opposite each other at the table, then she said, "I was praying this morning and God gave me a word for you". Now there was an opening to a conversation I had not heard before and was definitely not what I was expecting. Sure I had done a bit of praying in my time, let's be honest about it, when we are in trouble most of us think that it is worth giving this praying stuff a go. Hey, what is there to lose, if God is there and answers our prayers – result. If God isn't there, then who needs to know.

This was different, Lou was actually saying that God wanted to send me a message and she was being asked to deliver it, a bit like God's postwoman, or the angels I had read about in my youth who were sent to earth to deliver important messages to prophets or to Mary the mother of Jesus. Was I surprised? You bet I was. I was also intrigued, sceptical, scared, curious and part of me felt that maybe the plane had actually been hijacked and diverted after all – to the planet Zog. This was a slightly weird, no not slightly weird, a very weird situation.

I sat quietly waiting for this message then Lou said "God has told me to say that he has witnessed your struggle, and he is proud of you. he wants to assure you that he will never diminish you, he only asks that you never diminish him." That is the gist of the message, there was more to it than that, quite a lot more, but it is hard to remember it verbatim when you are sobbing like a baby. As Lou delivered this message, something inside of me broke and a sob forced its way up from the pit of my stomach and out of my mouth, tears streamed down my face, to complete my emotional reaction. Even in this state, a bit of my mind spoke to me saying, "You are really impressing her with your maturity and manliness, what must she think?"

So, what had happened? Those words seemed to speak to a deep yearning in me for recognition and appreciation. I did not even know that the yearning was there. I thought that I was strong, self-sufficient, independent, self-assured and did not need external affirmation (and many people who know me would say that this is true). But the words of this message penetrated deep inside and touched a hidden need, and it moved me profoundly. I have since come to learn that this kind of thing happens when you open yourself up to a relationship with God, so invest in tissues – you may get through a lot.

The problem for me was, at that time I was not in much of a relationship with God, at least not one that was as personal and intimate as this was. Sure I had kept God in the first aid cabinet, you never know when you might need either to fire off a few well-chosen prayers or to hedge your bets. But having a God that sent messages via an ex-girlfriend, now that was novel, and I wasn't sure how I felt about it!

Before continuing, I must give you some biographical information, so that you can understand what had just happened and what happened afterwards. The foundations of my relationship with God can be found in Lou's life and my life prior to this point. So the next few chapters will be a whistle stop tour through the time before Lou delivered God's message at the kitchen table.

2: My Family

Kirkintilloch, a small town about 10 miles from Glasgow, is ancient, tracing its roots back to before the Roman occupation of Britain. In fact, there is one theory that the name Kirkintilloch is Gaelic for "The fort at the end of the wall" which referred to one of the Roman forts in the Antonine Wall, built to hold back the wild Scots tribes that would sweep down from the hills. Certainly if you stand on the site of the fort, there is a wonderful view towards the Campsie Fells, a range of hills about three miles away. And if you stand there and let your imagination loose, you can just visualise the Highland hordes massing on those hills, readying themselves for an attack on the fort.

This town where I was born and grew up was small enough for people to know each other, or at least their families. It was the type of place that if you went to a party where there were a few generations, some of the older ladies were bound to ask, "Are you John's boy?" or "Are you Liz's grandson?". For Kirkintilloch people, it seemed to be important that they could place who you were, who your parents were and how long your family had been in Kirky (as the locals called it). For the purists, if you could call them that, if you moved to Kirky from elsewhere you could never become a Kirky person, no matter how long you lived there, to be a true Kirkintilloch person, you needed to be born there. I was born there, and so were my parents.

On the rare occasions that I go there today, I hardly recognise the place, as it has all changed so much over the last few decades. The 1960s started a huge transformation to the town, in the wake of the redevelopment of Glasgow. Many Glasgow residents found themselves uprooted and moved to new housing estates around central Scotland including Kirky. It happened because much of the sub-standard housing in Glasgow was being demolished. This influx of Glaswegians really changed the town in many ways, not just the size of the population but also its nature. Now there were lots of non-Kirky people. Kirky people were small town or country people, these incomers were city people who were accustomed to a much faster pace of life and many more shops and amenities. The Antonine Wall had fallen and the invasion had come, not as expected from the northern highlands, but from Glasgow in the southwest instead, and it changed Kirkintilloch forever.

My earliest memories are of our home in Kerr Street, just off Oxford Street (no, not that Oxford Street!!!), Oxford Street in Kirkintilloch. The flat was just off the main street (which was called Cowgate which probably harked back to its history of being a country village), so we lived almost in the centre of town. We had a small flat, what the locals would call a 'room and kitchen'. Characteristically this would be one room which was used as the bedroom, and a second room that fulfilled all the other functions of kitchen, dining and living room. The toilet was down an external staircase, in an outhouse in the garden, definitely not a place to linger in winter, as there was no heating and the toilet would regularly freeze up. Come to think of it, it wasn't a great place to linger in any other season either as it was dark, damp and was shared with assorted wildlife, most with far too many legs.

Living next door to us was a young couple, although at that time to me they seemed to be all grown-up. Occasionally they would babysit for me, if my parents needed to go out. Unfortunately, I can't remember anything much about them now, except an impression that they were a nice couple, who probably were better off than we were, as their house was better furnished and more modern than ours.

Upstairs there was an attic. This is where Robbie lived. Robbie was one of those people that adults spoke about in incomplete sentences like, "He was..., ye'know, again last night..." and with knowing looks and pained expressions and head shaking. This was my first introduction to word puzzles. What word or phrase fits the blank? Is it 1/ Happy 2/ Working or 3/ Drunk and incapable? Later when I got better at the puzzles, I found that the answer, at least when Robbie was involved, was nearly always number 3.

Unfortunately, I don't know much about Robbie, apart from him being the alcoholic in the attic. He was what we would think of as the stereotypical drunk, long wispy hair, shaggy beard and an old grey/brown overcoat tied shut with a piece of string. My mother and our neighbour took turns at taking him food, to make sure that he actually ate something at least once a day. Other than these food deliveries, we did not meet Robbie very often. He was a rather shadowy figure to me, coming home late from wherever he had been. Sometimes we were aware of him moving around above us and occasionally, when his demons were particularly bad, we would hear him shouting and arguing with them. But mostly he was harmless, a gentle but tortured soul.

I only remember being in Robbie's flat twice, as I was always warned to stay away from it. The first time was just after Robbie had been discovered dead and the authorities had removed the body. Then my mother and the neighbour had rolled up their sleeves to clean up the attic. It is one of my abiding memories of growing up, that people just seemed to accept responsibility for things that affected their lives. They did not start looking to see who they could unlike on Facebook, or who they could send a strongly worded email to with grumpy face emojis. They did not look to see who was going to come and sort things out, because they knew that the buck stopped at them, and so they just got on with it and did what was required of them.

While they were cleaning, I sneaked upstairs and peeked into the gloom that was Robbie's domain. It really did look like the local dump. There were bottles everywhere, empty of course! The floor was littered with papers and bits of rotting food plus the smell was awful. My mother chased me out to the garden to play while she and the neighbour set about the task of clearing up the debris of Robbie's sad life.

The second time I set foot in Robbie's flat was a few days later. The door was open and again I sneaked up the stairs. The sight that met me this time was so very different, my mother and the neighbour had worked their magic transformation. The bottles and the rubbish had all gone. Light shone in from the newly cleaned skylight onto the bare floorboards and the couple of little bits of furniture. The room was scrubbed, Robbie had gone, and so had all trace of him.

I have no idea what influence, if any, Robbie had on me then or since, but it is ironic that 30 years later my own flat should mirror the squalor of his attic. I find myself now wishing I knew more about him, who he was, where he came from and why he was so tortured, but sadly, any of the people I could have asked are gone. Nevertheless, I am so thankful that I was the one chosen to recover and survive.

One great amenity of our flat was the back garden. Because the building sat on a corner and bordered three roads, it had a large walled garden, making it a very safe place for children to play in. So, a few local kids around my age would come over to play in this garden. It was also a bit wild and unkempt, making it fun for us kids who would trek into the jungles of Africa, or fight great battles where the fate of the human race hung in the balance and we had to save the world yet again and all before teatime.

I can't say that I have a lot of vivid memories of that time, most of them are hazy, at best, and a couple of them have been embedded by talking to my mother and other relatives over the years. One memory I do have is of a three-legged tortoise that my dad and I had found outside our house. The poor thing had a crack on its shell and one leg missing, presumably as the result of a car accident. I took it home and let it loose in the wild hinterland of our garden and my imagination.

A couple of years ago, I came across an old black and white photo from that time. In the picture is myself and a couple of local kids around four or five years old, standing looking very solemn in that way that only kids can manage. I am in the middle dressed in a cowboy outfit, Stetson, guns in holsters and a sheriff star on my fancy waistcoat. When I asked my mother about the scene, she told me that the tortoise had died and I was officiating at its funeral. Clearly, it was a very fitting send-off for the tortoise as I, in my childish mind, obviously felt the need to dress appropriately for the occasion.

My Father

Let's start with a big statement. I believe my father loved me. However, sadly I never remember him actually saying it. In fairness to him, it was not the sort of thing that a West of Scotland man of his generation would say. West of Scotland men were hard, brooked no nonsense and had no time for frothy ostentations – like frilly shirts, flared trousers or emotions! Or at least, if they actually had any emotions, they were a well-guarded secret that no self-respecting member of that group would dare to air in public, not if they wanted to remain part of the club. They made the legendary inscrutability of the Chinese seem like an over sentimental melodrama.

I remember my father's funeral, as I lowered him into the grave, I shed a tear (well actually more than one), something you might expect to be natural and wholly appropriate in the circumstances. Suddenly I heard a hiss in my ear, "Stop that, be a man!" – it was my dad's older brother warning me that I was making an unseemly scene, by being sad. Being a next generation, recovering West of Scotland man, I expressed a few more emotions towards him that had him stomping off, shaking his head and wondering what the world was coming to.

Even though my father was not very expressive about his love for me, it seemed he did have genuine feeling for me. My mother told me that after she lost the children (more about that later) he refused to adopt. His reasoning being that it would not be fair to any adopted child, as he could never love someone else's child as much as he loved me. So, although he seems to have loved me deeply, he was not very demonstrative. In fact, my most enduring memories of him are of him telling me about his disapproval and disappointment. One of my main goals in this section is to examine my thoughts and feelings towards him and arrive at a more rounded, and probably (or hopefully) fairer, picture of him.

Back to our flat. Our little home sat above the British Legion Hall, which was a meeting place for military veterans. My father (a veteran himself) was part-time caretaker of this place, which meant that he would set up the hall for events and clear it up afterwards. When he was setting up or clearing away, I would often go down to the hall with him. At that time, I just wanted to be around him and do 'man things' with my dad. I seriously doubt if I was very helpful, as we lived there when I was between one and seven years old. However, I do remember that I learned to roller skate in that hall. It was a tiled floor, so it was great to skate on. And probably the biggest benefit was I could fall over in private and emerge from this skating cocoon as a competent skater at the end of the learning process.

His real job was a machinist, or to give it its proper title, a semi-skilled capstan setter operator. He had trained to do this job when he could no longer work at his trade which was a moulder and pattern maker in the local iron foundry. Moulding was a trade that was in high demand and very well paid, at least in comparison to most other trades. However, the fumes from the furnaces affected his stomach quite badly and made him ill. For most of his adult life he suffered from stomach ulcers and would regularly come home with the latest potion guaranteed to cure him. For weeks his mouth and lips would be black as he endured the regime of charcoal tablets, then the colour scheme would change to white or purple according to the latest 'cure' he was trying out. Unfortunately, nothing worked, or at least nothing brought relief on a long-term basis, but he was always optimistic. He was the type who would have been a ready and willing customer for any snake-oil salesmen of the Wild West.

Since working at his trade was not an option, it meant that he could not command tradesman wages. It did not matter that he was doing the same job, or that he probably did it better than many of those working beside him. If he did not have tradesman's papers for that job, he could not earn as much as those who did have them. They were the rules. And while I can understand the reason that had led to the trade unions negotiating those rules to protect tradesmen, it was difficult to see him walking out with considerably less money than the other men for the same amount of work. The result was that as a family, we never had a lot of money when I was growing up. However, I would not have considered us poor then, and still don't now. I can't say that I had a deprived or unhappy childhood, definitely not, but I was aware that many other kids had a bit, or sometimes a lot, more than us. They would go on holidays, some even went abroad, their dad had a car, they had a telephone or, a real biggie at the time, they had a TV. Eventually, we would get all these things, but others had them long before we did.

When I was seven years old, we moved to a brand-new house. The council had built a whole new estate on the edge of Kirkintilloch, and we moved into one of the last houses to be built there. This was a huge change, for now I had a bedroom all to myself and – this was really huge – we had an inside toilet with a real plumbed-in bath. We had gone from a tiny flat to an end of terrace two-bedroom house with up and down stairs. To us it was a mansion and, even better, everything was brand new. I loved it there. Although the estate was still a bit of a building site for a year or two, there were fields as far as you could see. We had a wonderful uninterrupted view over the fields to the Campsie Fells way in the distance. There were streams to fish, woods to roam, trees to climb and great hills for sledging in the winter. I could go out in the morning and roam for hours and never see another person. For me, it was a wonderful free place to grow up and, apart from the usual boyhood accidents such as falling in the stream, falling out of trees, falling down gullies (I seemed to have done a lot of falling) it was a very safe place to be a child. But back to my father.

After moving to this new house, he seemed to be in his element. He was a frustrated carpenter. As a boy he had wanted to become an apprentice cabinet maker but had been persuaded to sign on to be a moulder instead. But now we had a new house, he could indulge his dreams of building stuff with wood. One of the first projects was the shed, after all you can't do proper woodwork without a shed, a West of Scotland man needs a proper man cave. As the years passed, he became a hoarder, he saw everything as having potential: he would often say things like "That's a handy little tin" or "That bit of wood will come in handy" – "What for?" – "Oh, you never know when you'll need a bit of wood like that." So all of these 'handy things' found a home in the shed which eventually became a very dangerous place. Just opening the door could expose you to a possible avalanche of 'useful stuff.' Every couple of years we would clear it out but, somehow, it would very quickly become full again. Some of it was 'new' useful things and some of it 'rescued' stuff that he just could not bear to throw out, obviously because it could come in useful. The fact that its use had remained undiscovered all this time did not diminish his conviction that we needed to keep it somewhere safe. And no, John, the bin is not somewhere safe! One of the useful things he had was a selection of cobblers' lasts. Where he got them, I have no idea. But, having found them he decided that he was going to save the family loads of money by repairing all of our shoes. While I remember the lasts vividly, I can't remember any times when he actually used them for the purpose they were made for. The only purpose I remember was as door stops.

He attended a night school class for carpentry, which allowed him to indulge in his passion and where he could make furniture for the house. He started off small, making a stool and a little table. They were nicely made, he was clearly skilled and loved working with wood. The stool was something that we had for many years, until my mother moved house. One of his proud creations was a solid wood chess board for my chess phase. I still have it today, it is a lovely object, even though my chess phase passed many years ago. But his real masterpieces were the furniture that he built to fit in the recesses either side of the fireplace in the living room. These were very elaborate pieces of furniture, the centerpiece being a display cabinet with sliding glass doors. They were very impressive, and big, very big. When my mum moved to a one-bedroom house many years later, she took one of these pieces with her. The only way we could get it into this new flat was to take the front window out. After she died, sadly we had to break it up to get it back out. But while we were in that new house, they had pride of place and were admired, and maybe even envied, by everyone who came to visit.

Relationship with my Father

As I typed the heading for this section, I wondered whether to use the term dad or father. Dad felt too informal and father seems a bit staid. It is maybe a reflection of the relationship we had that I opted for the more formal father.

Like many children and parents, our relationship went through different phases over the years. Almost certainly this was mostly due to me and whatever was my current persona. In my childhood and early teens, we were close. Some of my most enduring memories were the trips we took on the Vespa scooter he had bought, as we couldn't afford a car at that time. Since a scooter had only two seats, these day trips were just me and my father. I loved these trips. We would head off into the countryside to places such as the Pots of Gartness, a pool in the river Endrick where salmon would gather before leaping the waterfall to swim upriver to spawn. This was magical for me, to see these magnificent fish overcome all natural obstacles in order to reach their spawning ground. On one of our visits, a salmon landed at my feet and one of the rangers who were there to protect the fish, shouted at me to put it back in the water. I felt a real thrill helping this wonderful creature to reach its goal. One of our favourite trips was through the Trossachs, a stunning area of natural beauty, full of lochs and mountains. After being introduced to it on these trips, this place became a real favourite place for me to visit after I learned to drive. When I was out with my father, on the way home, we would stop at a pub in Blanefield. He would disappear into this mysterious place reserved for adults, and I would be left sitting outside on a bench with a packet of crisps and a glass of lemonade. The outside of the pub had frosted glass advertising various beers, which meant that no one could see what was happening inside. At the time, I was curious about what happened in this forbidden place, what strange bonding rituals took place in the inner sanctum. I always had a vivid imagination. Maybe sitting on that bench wondering about what was happening inside sowed some seeds for my later relationship with pubs and alcohol, or on the other hand maybe not!

I loved these outings. It was just the two of us and the spectacular beauty of the Scottish countryside. To this day I love being among the Scottish mountains and the majestic scenery, and I owe that to him and these trips. What I do remember, although it never really struck me at the time, was that my father was someone who was happy to just look at the scenery. He was not someone who felt inclined to get off his scooter and off the road, to actually walk into this majestic countryside. It seemed that he just enjoyed whizzing through on his scooter, like Easy Rider. However, for me I wanted more of the countryside, so years later I would return to some of these places, but this time I would actually hike into the countryside and climb those mountains.

During my middle-to-late teens and into my early twenties our relationship could best be described as volatile. I was a child of the 60s, and I embraced it completely. I grew my hair long, very long, my clothes were clearly inspired by the hippy uniform and my taste in music became further and further from his – or even from the mainstream pop of the time. Rather than that kid who loved nothing better than to jump on the back of his scooter and head off into the hills, I did not want to spend any time with him. My view of him was he was wrong: about what – well, name the subject. Those years were difficult; we argued constantly about everything. Indeed, a few times my mother had to prevent us coming to blows.

In 1973, after I had been away from home for a couple of years, living the hippy life, I returned home for a short time before setting off again. However, when I returned home, I found that my father was unwell. True, he had been unwell much of my life, but this was different. The investigations showed that he had cancer of the stomach and the prognosis was in months, not years. Obviously, I could not head off again. Even I was not that selfish.

It may seem like a strange thing to say, but I will always be grateful for that time. All the things that we argued about, all the differences in our lifestyles, politics, music, beliefs, none of that seemed important. I became his chauffeur, his nurse, his companion, his son. Probably for the first time I saw him for who he was, a man. He was not just the person who was responsible for begetting me and looking after me as a child. He wasn't just the unreasonable person who disagreed with my lifestyle choices of living rough, taking drugs and getting drunk, he was someone who cared deeply for me. OK sometimes it was well hidden beneath his anger, like when he told me he was ashamed of me, or was disappointed in me, and there are many times I wish I could have wound the clock forward, so he could see the man I am today. But I am so glad we had that time, for during those few months we met as father and son, as men and, even if we did not say how much we loved each other, we at least demonstrated it by the way we treated each other. And I believe, even though he did not see the current me, he looked in my heart and saw the potential, at least I fervently hope that was the case.

My Mother

My mother was the second youngest of four surviving siblings. She had two older brothers and one younger sister. There had been other children (I don't know how many) who died in early childhood, the only one I know of was my namesake John, who died at around five years old. She was brought up in what would have been regarded as fairly comfortable circumstances. Her father (also John but everyone called him Jocky) was a moulder in the foundry, which was a well-paid job, and her mother Sarah was a housewife who looked after the children.

During the Second World War, my mother, like many women of her generation worked in munitions. For the last year of the war she was posted to Coventry to work in the large munitions factories there. While there she made some friendships that lasted all her life.

I remember her working for all my childhood, or at least as soon as I was at school. She had a variety of jobs, working in a greengrocer, a couple of petrol stations and as a dinner lady at my school, which was embarrassing, for me that is. Eventually her bosses realised that she was a good cook and sent her to train as a school cook. She worked in that capacity at the local primary school until she retired. My father and I reaped the benefit of this training, as her cooking, which had always been good, improved and her repertoire expanded.

When my father died, she was only 49 years old. So, it would not have been a great surprise to anyone if she had found a new love in her life or even a new husband. She was not short of offers. It's hard for a son to judge, but my mother although not a great beauty, was nevertheless an attractive woman. She was petite, five foot half an inch – she always insisted on the half inch – and she was slim and fit. However, she always said that she was not interested in another man, not after my father. I assume that she meant this in a good way, that is no one could ever replace the love that she had for him. And, true to her word, there was never anyone else in her life. She had some good friends and her sister lived nearby and she became very fond of lawn bowls, winning a few trophies and expanding her social circle.

Her funeral tea was held at the bowling club where she had spent many years. The club insisted. There was a huge turnout for her funeral as, apart from her couple of years in Coventry during the war, she had lived her whole life in Kirkintilloch. For me, it was lovely and touching to see how well-known and well-liked she was, that so many people would come to see her off. It was a side of my mother that I don't think I had ever actually known.

Relationship with my Mother

I think I have avoided writing this section, not knowing what to say. It might be a cliché to say that our relationship was complicated, but it was and, as I start writing this section, I realise it still is, even though she has been dead for many years. Maybe the process of writing it down will bring some clarity, hopefully.

I was my mother's firstborn, exactly nine months after their wedding, something that was more important and significant in those days. My parents were at great pains to reassure me that I was definitely a honeymoon baby. At birth, the medical staff did not rate my chances of living to be very high; apparently, I was very jaundiced and sickly. It seems that I could not eat, or at least could not keep anything down, so I started to lose weight. At the time we lived in a single room in a house with other families. One neighbour was a family called the Darrochs who had a gypsy background. Locally, the mother, Mamie, was considered to be a 'spey-wife' (a bit of a fortune teller and 'wise-woman') and it was she who helped my mother. The story goes that Mamie suggested the following: if I could not take nourishment by mouth then maybe I could receive it through my skin. So, every day she would rub my body with honey and herbs, and slowly I started to flourish and gain weight. Whether or not this is what actually happened I have no idea, I just know that this was the story I grew up with (pun definitely intended). Part of the reason that I had been a sickly child was that my mother had rhesus-negative blood type (negative because there was a protein missing from her blood) while my father was rh-positive. In the first child this difference is usually mostly harmless, but in subsequent pregnancies it can fatally damage the unborn child. The result was that my mother lost three children after me, so I was her only surviving child. Since that time, medicine has progressed enormously and treatment is readily available for this condition. Unfortunately, at that time there was no such treatment and my mother, who dearly wanted a larger family, was limited to just me.

One of my abiding memories happened when I was about nine or ten years old. When I see it now in my mind, it feels like an old tableau (where actors would pose for a dramatic scene). I am standing alone at the top of the garden (our garden was on a slope running down to the house). By the back door is my mother sitting in an armchair with a tartan rug wrapped round her legs. She is obviously grief stricken. Around her are her mother, her brother and sister and my father. They are trying to comfort her and have brought some presents. The reason for this gathering is that my mother has just come home from hospital having carried a stillborn baby to full term. This was the last of the three unsuccessful pregnancies that she had, and it had precipitated a severe bout of depression.

If you were a casual observer of this scene one of the things that might catch your eye is that, while there is a tight group round my mother, I am not part of the group. The reason for that was, I had been told to go away. It was not done out of callousness or cruelty. In that time, it was considered that being a child, either I would not understand, or I would not be affected by the tragedy that had occurred. So, all the focus was on my mother, who had lost a child. What no one understood was that I was also grieving, as I had lost a sibling, and not just one. I had deeply felt the loss of the other two also.

Later that same day I was packed off to live with my aunt and cousins, as my mother could not cope with life, never mind looking after a child. I stayed there for about six months until she recovered. In some respects, I enjoyed living there. I had always been desperate to have a brother or sister. Watching other kids go home together always left me feeling envious. So, while staying with my cousins Archie and Maria was great, it was also a mixed blessing. I loved being there with them and they made me very welcome. But I always knew it was a temporary arrangement, that I was not a 'real' member of the family and also, I missed my parents and my own home.

In recent years I have come to realise that the trauma of that time has had a more profound effect than I, or anyone else, realised. On the one hand I felt that I was a burden that needed to be shed for at least a little while. On the other hand I sensed that I was 'not enough'. Even writing these words feels so selfish, but I have to remember it was a child that felt these hurts, and being excluded from the family grief just seemed to emphasise them. At the time I did not understand, or could not have articulated, any of this. And while I understand it better now as an adult, I am not writing this to accuse or blame anyone. No, I am offering it as a partial explanation of some of my later feelings about my self and the subsequent behaviour – more on this later.

Not surprisingly, after her losses, my mother became over-protective throughout my childhood and, indeed, most of my life. This was problematic for her as I was an extremely independent child, the more she tried to 'protect' me the more I tried to express my freedom. In fact I had first exerted my independence when I was around three or four. I packed a packet of crisps and a biscuit into the saddlebag of my tricycle and headed off for a round-the-world adventure. Some neighbours in the next street intercepted me and returned me to my parents. This was a tension that lasted most of her life. I still remember vividly two of the most notable examples of her controlling over-protection.

The first was when she approached the headmaster of our high school to discuss my education. I had just received the results of my eleven-plus. This was the test that decided what classes and subjects one would study at secondary school. Students were graded as A – the top stream studying academic subjects, through B, C and D becoming progressively less academic and more technical. I was one of only six A-stream students from our school. When the results arrived, my mother quickly arranged an appointment with the headmaster and proceeded to demand that I be downgraded to the B-stream. Her rationale was I might become over stressed if I was too stretched by the curriculum. The headmaster was flabbergasted. He told her that he had parents coming to him regularly begging for their child to be upgraded, that this was the first time in his experience that a parent had come and asked for their child to be downgraded. He then proceeded to tell her that my exam scores had been the highest in the county, not just the school and he therefore refused her request.

The second example came when I was 16 years old. Being a strong swimmer, I had become captain of the school swimming team. Our school had an annual pool gala where the four houses of the school would compete against each other. The climax of the gala was the relay race. I was swimming the anchor leg of the relay, but my teammates had fallen far behind and left me with a large deficit to make up. When the third swimmer of our team touched the pool, I dived in and gave it everything I had. On the first length of the pool I started to make up the ground and on the second length I was clearly catching the others. The crowd were cheering me on as I managed to overtake each of the other houses and finish in first place. It was a great moment for our house and a real moment of glory for me. However, unknown to me, rather than cheering for me to catch the others, my mother was actually shouting for me to slow down – in case I hurt myself! People around her could not believe her attitude and even today, I still can't believe it.

It is not too difficult to imagine how this over-protective control would clash with my fiercely independent spirit and often lead to friction. Indeed, the more my mother tried to control what I did, the more I tried to exert my independence. Looking back now, it may even have been a factor in my going to the seminary. It was certainly part of the reason that I was happy there, free of her influence. Although a major part of that happiness came from the feeling of being in a large family, something that I felt the need for deeply.

The scars of my childhood were deep and complex, yet I was mostly unaware of them until much later in life. In hindsight, however, they clearly did underlie much of my behaviour and how I interacted with the world. My mother's depression at losing the last of the children set in me a belief that I was not enough. Why could she not just be happy with me? That belief was further compounded by her over protectiveness which gave me feelings that I was not good enough – to be in the top class at school, to win a swimming race. At the time, I had no idea that these feelings were taking very deep root in me. Indeed it was not until later in life that I realised that my behaviour could be traced back to some of these incidents in my childhood. After my father died the tension between my mother and me heightened. Having suffered yet another loss, my mother's fear of even more loss was projected onto me all the more. She wanted to know everything about where I was going, who I would be with and when I would be back. Having spent more than half of the previous ten years living away from home (the seminary and as a hippy) I found these restrictions extremely difficult. However, I also need to say that, at that time I was too self-absorbed to recognise her pain or fears. I just wanted to get on with my life of sex, drugs and rock 'n' roll without having to answer to anyone, and definitely not to an over-protective mother. So, we both retreated into our respective cocoons of absolute certainty of what we considered to be right and reasonable. An uneasy truce with occasional sporadic arguments became the pattern of our relationship.

3: Are Your Pants Clean?

My parents were not particularly devout, but they were active observers of the laws of Catholicism. One real benefit was that you knew where you were with Catholicism. There was a well-defined scorecard that told you whether you were in credit or debit in the Bank of Heaven. Attended mass this Sunday, tick; been to confession this year, tick; taken communion this year, tick; abstained from meat on Friday, tick; no unconfessed mortal sins – ah, that's a bit more tricky.

The point was that if you had enough ticks on Sunday then you could spend the rest of the week feeling relaxed. As a fully ticked up member of the Catholic church you could rest in the sure knowledge that, if you were to die at that moment you would be transported instantly to Heaven. Well, maybe not instantly, you might have to spend a few million years in Purgatory, but at least you were not going to Hell, and that was the important thing.

My impression of religion, particularly when I was young, was that you had to live your life defensively. Priests and teachers seemed to spend a lot of time talking about the state of your soul when you die. It felt a lot like we were walking a tightrope stretched across the pit of Hell and at any moment we could plunge into the oblivion of eternal damnation. Not a comfortable feeling.

My mother, like many mothers before, during and since her, was always checking to see that my pants and vest were clean going into school. This inspection was not really borne of an obsession for hygiene. No, it was in case that I was run over by a car and killed on my way to school, and a subsequent inspection were to find that I was – Oh the shame of it – wearing dirty pants. Although you have to say that the logic is a bit flawed as, if I were to see this fatal car coming, I very much doubt that the pants would stay clean very long. And you have to ask, would my mother's grief have been lessened if I went to meet my maker with clean underwear. I can just hear the neighbours "It was a tragedy that he was killed, but wasn't it such a blessing that he died with spotless Y-Fronts. His mother must be so proud, she is such a wonderful woman."

To me in my pre-teens, being a Catholic felt very much like the clean pants scenario, as I often imagined God, or my guardian angel saying, "I hope that you have a clean soul going out there. What would become of you if you got knocked down on the way to school?" No wonder when I imagined God talking to me, he usually sounded very much like my mother, but with a deeper voice, and a bit more Jewish sounding obviously, but otherwise the things he said tended to be very similar.

Anyone growing up as a Scottish Catholic in the 50s and 60s learned three things: existential fear, guilt and bigotry. Existential fear is a non-specific fear or anxiety that something bad is going to happen (e.g. being knocked down on the way to school), or even worse, it has already happened and we don't know about it. To put it another way the world was a hostile place full of traps and nasty things for the unwary. Growing up in the West of Scotland this was summed up in the often quoted saying "Life is hard and then you die." You have to admit, we Scots are a very cheerful nation.

Then there was the guilt. Like the existential fear, it seemed that there was very little that we could take pride in, and plenty that we needed to be ashamed of. If we were ever to forget that we were sinners, there were plenty of people around that were only too happy to remind us; for example teachers, neighbours, aunts and most adults. Indeed, that seemed to be their principal occupation – guilt inducers! There was also a lot of talk about sin and its various varieties. There was original sin, we were born with that one, as we had inherited it from Adam and Eve eating one of their five a day from the wrong tree. Then there was venial sin, a kind of misdemeanour which God could forgive. Venial sins were everywhere, thinking bad things about someone, telling lies (white ones obviously), not doing what parents, teachers or almost any adults told you to do, all came under the heading of venial sins. For a while I felt you could not wake up in the morning before starting your venial sin tally for the day.

Mortal sin though was the bad one. If you died without having confessed a mortal sin then it was a one-way trip to Hell, with no reprieve. As a child I was terrified that I would be run over by a bus wearing dirty underpants and having a mortal sin on my soul. I was not sure whether God had a special hell for this double offence, or whether the wearing of dirty underpants was a mortal sin in its own right anyway.

I wish that I had known then what I know now, it would have saved me a lot of my childhood worry and guilt. What I now know is that God is my Father who loves me and wants me to be with him and be safe. But, because he is holy and righteous, he hates sin and someone needs to pay for all that sin. But rather than being a big scary God who just wants to punish us, he sent Jesus to save me from the consequences of sin. So if I give my life to Jesus, then when God looks at me, he sees a clean soul, not because I have been a good person and never sinned, but because Jesus' sacrifice on the cross has paid for all my sins, original, venial and even mortal ones. That means that I don't need to live in fear, as my debt of sin is paid and if that bus knocks me down then I'm not going to go to Hell. Ah but, as for the underpants, I'm afraid that's a completely different story, a bit too complicated for my limited theology.

Bigotry

It might sound strange but I was not really very aware that I was a Catholic until I started school. Before that, I had a small group of friends that would come round the garden where we would play all the usual children's games, hide and seek, Cowboys and Indians and just general running and screaming, very popular when I was younger. Obviously, since we were all around the age of five, there was not a lot of deep and meaningful theological discussions about religion or comparative discourses regarding Catholicism and how it related to the Protestant movement. No our discussions tended to centre more around whether worms were good to eat or who would win a fight between a dragon and a shark. In case you want to know, obviously it is the dragon, even though Protestants think that the shark would win. Ah is there no end to their heresy!

Where I lived, just off Oxford Street, there was a cinema *(The Pavilion)* across the road and a primary school slightly further up where all my little friends went. Come the day I started school, I thought that I would go to that school as well. However, instead I was marched past this school and taken to another school, about half a mile away, which was a bit puzzling for a child not quite five years old. That day John passed the school across the road as a friend and when he returned he had turned into a f*****g pape (an extremely derogatory term for Catholics) and found that his little friends were now 'proddy dogs' (the derogatory term for Protestants).

That day I had unknowingly been initiated into the murky world of bigotry and sectarianism, and found out that we needed to participate in the ancient ritual of hating each other. However, if you are going to have a really efficient system of bigotry then what is needed is a way of readily identifying who was on your side (the ones who were in the right) and the others (i.e. the heretics). Thankfully, the school system had thought this through and dressed us in brightly coloured school blazers, so we could readily identify the enemy from a distance. Our (Catholic) blazers were brown with blue braiding and the heretics wore grey blazers with green braiding; it would have been difficult to come up with more contrasting uniforms. Now the sides were clear and the targets for our insults, kicks and stones were readily identifiable, just in case we should harm anyone through friendly fire.

After a week or so, my little friends came back to the garden and we played our games again. The sectarian 'war' was left outside, well most of the time that is. Though, we found that whenever there was an argument, like a disputed goal at football or who's turn it was to be the teacher or the sheriff, we now had the explanation for that kind of behaviour – it was because they were proddies. Although, inexplicably they, the proddies, were sometimes delusional and thought that I might be in the wrong because I was a pape.

The biggest, most ostentatious display of sectarianism happened annually, on the 12th of July. Every year in towns all over the West of Scotland and Northern Ireland the Orange Order would have its annual parade – The Orange Walk – to commemorate Prince William's victory at the Battle of the Boyne in 1690. William, who became King William III defeated the Jacobite army of the deposed Catholic King James II who was trying to regain the British throne. The march is accompanied by bands, often very accomplished musicians, who play lots of sectarian and anti-Catholic songs like F*** the Pope! Ironically, the pope of the time, Alexander VIII, was in fact an ally of William (or King Billy as he is usually known) and supported his cause; not a fact that is either widely known or acknowledged in Orange circles.

The event, with its bands and the banners, is probably a quaint and colourful spectacle to a tourist, but to locals it is a highly emotionally charged event, on both sides. Often heavy drinking is involved and, because of the militant nature of the march, there is at least a sense or a threat of, if not actual, aggression and violence. Although sometimes that aggression actually spills over into violence, on both sides.

Every day was not a battle. I would have said at the time, and still do say, that I had a happy childhood. When you grow up with sectarianism you don't recognise it as such. It is just a normal part of life, part of the scenery. People just accept that this is the way things are, the way they have always been and probably always will be. It is like living in an echo chamber, all the voices are saying the same thing – and what they are saying is, this is normal. Sometimes it would raise its ugly head in ways that were difficult to ignore, like the Orange March or being chased home from school by proddies. But most days, especially as a child, you did not notice it too much.

One expression of this sectarianism could be found in the not-so-subtle rituals that would be enacted if you brought a friend home for the first time, even less subtle if it was a girlfriend. In these cases parents, mostly mothers, would ask the big question – "And what school do you go to?" If the answer did not contain a saint's name or some religious reference like The Sacred Heart Academy or Blessed Mary Comprehensive, there would be a very awkward silence. And by awkward, I mean almost palpable, deafening even. I suppose there was a similar ritual going on in Protestant houses, although I don't actually know. All I do know is that Catholic mothers could teach the KGB lessons on how to interrogate. And forget the monarchs, the real Defenders of the Faith were these West of Scotland Mothers ensuring that no heretic got through the net to pollute their family tree by marrying their sons or daughters. And that was almost certainly as true of Protestants as it was of Catholics.

This deeply engrained bigotry seemed to have some strange rules. It was OK (maybe nigh on compulsory) to hate Protestants, after all they hated you as a Catholic, and they were all bound for Hell anyway. However, it was not OK to hate your Protestant neighbour or friend. They were all lovely, generous people, fellow Scots; even though, and it goes without saying, you would not want your son or daughter to marry one! There are limits to Christian love, and that is most definitely beyond the pale.

An incident that happened when I was about twelve years old really illustrated the seriousness of this religious divide to me. My paternal grandfather, Hughie, had died and I was the altar boy at his funeral. As the pallbearers were putting his coffin into the hearse, I noticed three men standing across the road. They were very distinctive. Two of them were older, about the same age as my grandfather and the third was younger. What made them stand out was that although they were dressed in black coats, their clothes were clearly expensive. They all stood very solemnly with their hats in their hands and their heads bowed. This obviously piqued my interest, so after the funeral I asked my dad who they were. His answer was a bit of a shock even then.

I can't say if the story he told me was completely accurate, but he certainly believed it and I had no reason then or now to doubt what he told me. My grandparents, on both my mother's and father's side were second generation Irish immigrants and Catholics, part of the large influx in the mid-19th Century escaping the potato famine. However, Scotland was not as welcoming as they hoped, especially if you were a Catholic. Whether or not it was actually a Kirkintilloch bylaw, in the early 20th Century, it seems that no Catholics owned property in the higher west side of the town. This meant that most of them lived in the lower east side where two rivers met and regularly flooded. In the Kirkintilloch Museum there are many photographs of these floods showing the devastation that many of the inhabitants of that area suffered.

My grandfather and his two brothers had decided that they could pool their savings and become businessmen, make some money for their families and also help some of these poorer families in the accommodation at risk of flooding. What they were going to do was to buy and renovate property in the higher west side of Kirkintilloch and rent it to Catholics. They were going

46 / No Cloistered Life

to become landlords. But this proved to be very difficult for them as they came up against all the prejudice directed at immigrants, especially Catholic immigrants. My grandfather's two brothers decided that the way to overcome this prejudice was "if you can't beat them, join them". That is, they became Protestants, and so now they were free of the stigma of Catholicism, they prospered.

These were the men across the road at my grandfather's funeral; they were his two brothers and his nephew. Seemingly back when they proposed their solution to the prejudice to my grandfather, he refused to go along with them and they were ostracised from the family. I never knew anything about it because this 'betrayal' was hardly ever mentioned, and when it was mentioned, it was spoken of in whispers. It was almost like listening to a horror story about someone who had been abducted never to be seen again. My understanding is that my grandfather never spoke to his brothers again, because they had 'turned their coats', and worst of all, they did it for money. Over the years they had clearly prospered, while he became a miner who went through extremely hard times financially and health wise.

Even though Kirkintilloch was a small town, I never met the brothers again. They had come to say goodbye to their brother. But even this had to be done at a distance, as no one in the family would acknowledge they existed, never mind welcome them to the wake. I did meet their son about ten years later. I was standing at a bus stop in Kirkintilloch when a man about my father's age came and said, "I'm your cousin." There was not much more to the conversation as my bus arrived. When I arrived home, I told my mother about the strange encounter. "Oh that would have been Con. He is your dad's cousin. But we don't speak about them."

And that was the end of that. It showed me the divisive power of religion, even on my own family, family that I had not known and, apart from these small glimpses, have never known.

How do you explain this kind of division to people who have no experience of it? Sure, lots of families have rifts, about all sorts of slights, real or imagined, but the attitudes and behaviour in regard to religion have a particularly toxic quality in the West of Scotland. I was to find out one day in the summer of 1974 just how abnormal these attitudes were.

That year, on Saturday lunchtimes, a few friends and I had started going to a pub that we called the 'squeeze box shop'. We called it that because a guy would come in and play an accordion and the customers would have a bit of a sing along, sometimes all together, sometimes solo. The accordionist was a very accomplished musician and would play requests for anyone who wanted to sing a particular song. Today it would probably be a karaoke machine, but it was a lot less hi-tech then.

When we first started going to the pub the locals were understandably a bit wary. What they saw was half a dozen guys in their early twenties, long hair and dressed like hippies invading their cosy little pub. The locals were all much older and very conservative. However, after we had been there a few times, they realised that we were just there to enjoy the atmosphere and the music, so they welcomed us. In fact, I think that they actually enjoyed us being there, maybe they thought that it made the pub seem cool. Or then again maybe not!

That day Anne, my friend Eddie's girlfriend, had come to visit from Leeds. So, on the Saturday we thought that we would introduce her to a bit of culture, Glasgow style. Off to the 'squeeze box shop' we went for an afternoon of drinking and singing. As usual we were all singing along with the music and enjoying the usual warm atmosphere when the doors opened. A crowd of people dressed in the regalia of the Orange Order came in. The change in the pub's atmosphere was instant and dramatic.

It felt like someone had turned on a huge and very powerful air conditioning unit. Then one of the girls from this group asked the accordionist to play a song – The Banks of the Ohio by Olivia Newton-John. There was a collective sigh of relief, a nice poppy sing-along tune. Wrong, when she started singing, the lyrics had obviously been changed to The Barricades of the Shankhill Road. Oh dear! If there had been a collective shiver through the pub when they first came in, now there was an audible groan as she belted out the sectarian lyrics about the Irish troubles. And leaving no one in any doubt about where she and her companions stood on the question. So, we decided to leave and go somewhere a bit more peaceful.

Anne just looked at us and said, "What is happening?"

We just finished our drinks and left to go to the pub round the corner. When we got there she asked, "Well what was all that about? What happened?"

"It's the Orange Walk today, that's what was happening." "Sorry, what are you talking about?"

"You know, it's the Orange Walk." Anne just looked at me as if I was speaking in some strange exotic dialect. In fact the more I tried to explain the concept of the Orange Order, the sectarianism and bigotry, all things that we routinely took for granted, the more I realised that she had absolutely no idea what I was talking about.

She looked at our small group and asked, "Are you all Catholics?"

"Well no, half of us are, the rest are Protestants."

"If Catholics and Protestants hate each other, then how come you are friends."

"Ah well, we're pals – we know each other, have done for years. It might be different if we didn't know each other."

"So, what you're saying is that you can hate Protestants that are strangers, but if you have been introduced then you like each other. Is that right?"

"I wouldn't put it quite like that."

"How would you put it?"

"You're a Catholic, aren't you?"

"Yes, I was brought up as a Catholic."

"And you went to a Catholic school?"

"No, I didn't. I just went to the local school with everybody else, Catholics, Protestants, Muslims, Hindus and anybody else. There were no single religion schools, we just got on with it."

Clearly she could not understand the religion issue, despite all our explanations. It was a bit like trying to explain to a blind man the subtle differences in the tartans of two clans. For us, seeing it through the eyes of someone who is a stranger to the culture served to highlight the madness of sectarianism. It was a real eye-opener for us, at least it certainly was for me. I should say here that things have changed since the 1970s. I can't say that bigotry has disappeared completely, it is just less overt and more nuanced than it was.

Back then, if this incident did anything for me, it was to make me even less interested in religion. But before that I had been very interested in God and religion. Indeed, it played a major role in my life.

4: Understanding God

The title for this chapter triggers in me the temptation to stop there and leave the rest of the pages blank. I mean how can I possibly understand God, is that not really presumptuous? Not that something like that would usually deter me, I often fall into presumption. In fact I often believe that I know better than God does about how he should behave, especially regarding anything concerning me. Another reason I was tempted to leave it blank is because my understanding of God is not a fixed system of belief, it is a wonderful, surprising journey of discovery, where he reveals more of himself and, in the process, more about me. But regardless of how valid these reasons might be, a blank chapter, however deeply philosophical and symbolic, makes for dull reading.

    I should issue a warning here, if you are looking for a theological treatise here, then you will be disappointed. This is not a chapter of theology, at least not in the conventional sense we generally accept, i.e. an academic study of God. What it does represent is my own personal encounters with God and the story of me getting to know him in his many facets. It has been, and continues to be, a truly fascinating experience. Recently I have had to unlearn much of my previous belief system, that had come from the beliefs and dogma of others. Then I had to accept a completely new concept of God as a being, who not only interacts with us, but loves to do so. Now isn't that amazing! I'm still trying to get my head round it.

Early memories of God

Growing up in a Catholic household, I was always aware of God, or more accurately symbols of God. All round the walls there were 'holy pictures' such as the Sacred Heart of Jesus, the Child of Prague and, of course, the plaster statue of Mary, Mother of Jesus, who is such a big favourite of Catholics everywhere. Where modern households tend to have photos of the family graduating, getting married, or on the victor's podium of the egg and spoon race, we had the saints and the various representations of Jesus.

I didn't have the impression that having these pictures and statues around the house made me feel any closer to God or the saints. However, it did make me feel that I was under surveillance all the time. This made me feel even more guilty in my adolescence when I discovered the hobby of masturbation, which meant that I had to either cover the photos or turn the statues towards the wall, so that they could not see and accuse me. But it never really worked as they always looked very disapproving when I turned them back again.

Guilt seemed to be a prominent and enduring emotion as I grew up in a Catholic household. It always figured especially strongly during Lent, particularly when we were marched from school in our classes to our local church, to hear the White Fathers preach. The White Fathers were missionaries to Africa, but every so often they were sent to preach at churches back in the UK. When I first saw them, I thought that they looked exciting, romantic figures. They were dressed in long flowing white robes that contrasted beautifully with their tanned, weather-beaten look. Plus, they were out there bringing savages and cannibals to God (back then that's how I saw their role, forgive me I was young). I wanted to be one of them, although on reflection, I think it was mainly for the cool uniform and spending time in the sun. I was less sure about meeting savages (especially the cannibals) and the religious aspects of the role.

When they spoke though, there was not much romance. They sounded like Old Testament prophets who were having an especially grumpy day, as they preached about Hell and damnation for sinners like us. I wanted to jump up and shout "I'm only six, why do I need to go to Hell?" I was terrified, many of my classmates were crying, some just whimpered and wanted their mum, one poor boy even wet himself in fear. It was mayhem, we just huddled together for protection, as this priest delivered the pronouncement of our fate. God did not feel very cosy or comforting that day, he felt cruel and vindictive and just waiting for me and my classmates to sin in thought, word or deed! He had it all covered, there was no hiding place, not even inside your own mind. I really did not want to meet this God.

Fortunately, the clever old Catholic Church had thought of that, and put a system in place that meant that I did not need to meet with or talk to God. My childish understanding of the situation was that we paid someone else to do it for us, we called them priests. The contract seemed to be that we put money into the collection plate, and they stood out there in the firing line between God and us. Also (when I was young) they spoke in Latin, so not only did we not have to talk to God, we did not even need to understand the conversation the priests had with God, just in case we happened accidentally to overhear it. So, since clearly God spoke Latin, even if he had spoken to me, I would not have understood a word he said. As a child, it seemed like a very good, well thought out system to me. It meant that you could go into a church anywhere in the world and have exactly the same experience of not knowing what was going on, just as if you were at home.

As I mentioned in the previous chapter, starting school was the first time I became aware of being a Catholic, and that I was different from many of my neighbours. Opposite where we lived was a cinema and a primary school. The cinema I would spend a lot of my childhood in, the primary school, I would never set foot in. You see, that school was for Protestants and I had to go to the Catholic school that was half a mile away. At five years old I found it difficult to understand why all my little friends went there and yet I had to walk past it and hike that extra half mile. However, that was the system in the West of Scotland. Catholics went to Catholic schools, full stop, no argument.

Hello this is God Calling

When I got a bit older, about nine or ten, I found myself drawn to be an altar boy, someone who helps the priests when they celebrate Mass, officiate at funerals or any of the other services that were part of the priest's duties. Again, maybe it was the uniform that attracted me (is there a dressing up theme emerging here?), maybe it was my desire for attention, I don't remember now. What I do remember was that I was proud to be an altar boy and I loved carrying out my role with, as I believed, a bit of flair while the congregation watched and admired my performance. I really perfected the pious face (a bit like the expression you get when trying desperately not to fart at a formal event).

Our parish priest recognised that I was a quick learner so, after about a year or so I was promoted and given the task of teaching some of the new altar boys. At that time (late 1950s to around 1964) the Tridentine Mass was still practised. That is the Mass was still celebrated in Latin, with the priest facing away from the congregation. So the altar boys needed to learn the prayers and responses in Latin. My job then was to teach them the Latin responses and how to assist the priest e.g. serving him with the water and wine, having any books (Bible, New Testament, Prayer Books) available for him when required. This was a role that I enjoyed, it gave me some authority and made me feel important.

Another aspect of the altar boy role, this I enjoyed a lot, was that sometimes it took you out of the church to interesting places. Every Sunday, one of the priests had to go and say Mass at the local psychiatric hospital and then again at the local convent, and one of us altar boys would have to go with him. It was always fun if you were picked to go. The hospital was a bit scary to local kids who had grown up hearing the horror stories about the 'asylum' up the road. Not that anything ever happened to me, or anyone I knew, but there was always someone who knew somebody that knew somebody that had visited the 'asylum' and had never been seen again!

Mass would take place in the big hall, which was used for any gatherings and would be attended by about 150 patients and staff. Once it was finished, I would be left to clear everything away while the priest went off to visit anyone who was physically sick and also be available for anyone who wished to make their confession. Then came the bit that we loved: one of the perks of going to the hospital was the breakfast. At that time Woodilee Hospital had a 500-acre farm with reputedly one of the best dairy herds in the district. So all the produce for the breakfast came from the farm. It was fresh, plentiful and a great treat, as our plates were heaped with bacon, black pudding, eggs and mushrooms – wonderful!

After breakfast, we would head off to the convent, and again the priest would say Mass and I would assist. This was a stranger affair, as this was a closed convent. That meant that most of the nuns were cloistered, so they were behind a kind of filigree screen. You were aware of people being there but could neither see them nor even tell how many people were there. There were also two sisters who were not cloistered, they were the link with the outside world. They shopped for the convent and did anything that required a public presence. However, any important decisions tended to be made by the Mother Superior. When mass was finished, as in the hospital, the priest would be available for confession and anyone who was sick while I cleared away. The public nuns would then pounce on me and try and feed me with scones and cakes. Sometimes, to their disappointment I would only have room for a few of each, so they would send me on my way with a doggy bag.

Occasionally, Mother Superior would ask to see me. It was slightly surreal talking to her through this lattice screen. Although on these occasions I always felt a bit intimidated by this godly woman, I also felt a genuine warmth and affection coming from her. She may have been shut away from the world physically, but she was very much aware of what was going on outside. In these meetings she always asked about my life and my family and the next time we met she always remembered what I had told her. It is easy for us to believe that cloistered nuns are escaping from the world and have no interest in it, but five minutes with this woman dispelled that myth. She was very interested in the world, as well as being herself very interesting.

Soon being an altar boy was not enough; I wanted to be the priest. In hindsight I could easily dismiss this desire as merely wanting to be the star of the show, rather than a supporting act. However, although there may be some truth in that, it would definitely not be the whole story. I truly felt at the age of twelve that God was calling me to become a priest, that he wanted me to dedicate my life to him. My parents were not convinced at all. In fact, they (especially my mother) said that I was far too young to make that kind of decision and tried to dissuade me. However, I was determined and stubborn as a boy (still am) and so I recruited the help of the parish priest, who brought the bishop and under the pressure of all this clergy, my mother, being a good Catholic woman, had little option but to reluctantly concede. So aged thirteen, I packed my trunk and headed to the seminary on, what I saw as, the first steps to becoming the first ever Scottish pope. I knew that it was only a matter of time until I became 'Pope Hamish I.'

I loved the seminary right from the beginning. Being an only child, it gave me a large family of brothers that I always longed for but had never had. Many of the kids there cried at night, because they were homesick and missed their mum. I never did. From the beginning, I felt that this was where I wanted to be. To me it felt natural, it felt like home. The seminary was basically a boys' boarding school with religious overtones, a kind of Hogwarts for budding priests, but, unfortunately, with more hymns and fewer mythical beasts.

In Scotland there were two different seminaries. The first was St Vincent's College in Langbank, which sat on the Clyde estuary and catered for boys from 12 to 14, i.e. the first two years of secondary school. The second, St Mary's College, Blairs near Aberdeen, catered for the next four years of secondary school. I started in Langbank at 13 for one year and then moved to Blairs for the next two years, leaving at 16.

A typical day started at 7 a.m. with lights on. All the boys would rise, wash, dress, make up their beds and make their way to the chapel for morning Mass, all in silence. (All religious houses, and a seminary was one, observed the Grand Silence, which meant that, apart from an emergency, no one spoke from 10p.m. at night until after the reading at breakfast, usually around 8.30). We would attend Mass in the chapel and then make our way to the refectory for breakfast. One of us boys would read from the selected spiritual book of the week and when he was finished, the Grand Silence was over, and we could talk to each other again. After breakfast there would be classes, then lunch, with more readings. In the afternoon there might be more classes or maybe sport, depending on the season that could be football, cricket, or in the winter months, sledging. Then in the evening we would have dinner, then there was free time before prayers, the Grand Silence and bed.

I was in my element in this place, especially as it sat in the centre of a huge farm. So there were fields and woods to roam around. Every week there were sports for three half days. In the summer we had cricket, and in the winter it was football, or occasionally shinty. However, being in the north of Scotland winter often brought snow, lots of snow. Then we had sledging and mass snowball fights, where a lot of grudges were settled in a 'controlled' environment.

I was considered pretty wild in the seminary. However, let's put things in perspective, it was a seminary with lots of boys who wanted to be priests! You did not have to try very hard to get a reputation, you could have waged a reign of terror with a balloon on a stick. In saying that, the college ran a demerit system. Prefects would report any breach of the rules which each had a tariff: one demerit for a trivial offence, three for something more serious and six for the most serious offences. On a Sunday evening the whole college would assemble in the study hall and all demerits were read out, so there was a ritualistic element of shaming involved. The number of demerits that a student had accumulated over the term were subtracted from the end of term exam results, so passing the exams and being allowed to continue at the college was dependent not only on academic performance but also on behaviour. During my stay, I had the very dubious distinction of having the highest ever number of demerits recorded. There was nothing particularly serious. It was more a case of having a rebellious attitude, I never really could cope too well with authority, particularly anything that I, in my great wisdom, deemed to be petty bureaucracy, which were most rules that I did not like. Fortunately for me, my academic performance more than compensated for my behavioural lapses, so I was not really in danger of being thrown out.

The only particularly mischievous thing that I did, happened in my second winter in Blairs. The senior boys (years five and six) had their private skating pond and were very possessive about it. That is, they would not allow us juniors to enjoy it. So one evening when no one was around, myself and a couple of my fellow juniors decided to sabotage it. The pond had a drainage pipe at one corner, to allow the water to be drained, which is exactly what we did. We removed the pipe and most of the water poured out leaving the ice completely unsupported. Later when the seniors came to indulge in a bit of skating, the ice collapsed, leaving a couple of very wet, very cold and very angry seniors, and a skating pond beyond repair for the rest of the season. No one could prove it was me that did it, but a lot of seniors had very strong suspicions, and they made sure that they worked out their grudges on me during the next snowball fight.

As you would expect in a seminary, there were plenty of religious services. Mass was a daily occurrence, as was Evening Prayer. There were also Stations of the Cross, devotions and other assorted prayer meetings and services, all of these were weekly, monthly or seasonal. Every day there were readings from a religious book, say the life of a saint, and of course we had religious instruction as part of the curriculum. For me, and I can't speak for others, most of these services had a very ritualistic aspect to them. They felt like a performance and when I was part of them, I felt that I was much more aware of my peers and masters watching me, than I was of God watching me. It was more important to get the words or actions correct and particularly adopting a suitably pious expression (think of somewhere between sucking on a lemon and constipation), than it was to connect with God. After all, God could see my heart, but my peers could only see my face.

The only time I felt a genuine spiritual encounter, was during the retreats. These retreats usually lasted one or three days, not sure why there were no two-day retreats. During these times the school functions of the seminary were suspended, so there were no classes or sport. All the usual services were observed, and the Grand Silence was extended to the whole day with a short break after supper and before bedtime. These may sound like difficult times, but I loved them, especially the three-day retreats. For me, it felt that I was given time and space to be by myself, and to be myself. Although I loved being in the seminary and being part of a big family, there was, and still is, a part of me that craved solitude at times. Maybe that is the legacy of being an only child, or maybe it is because I'm a raving introvert; whatever the reason, the retreats gave me that space that I sometimes craved.

But it did not just give me space and solitude. It gave me time to reflect on why I was in this place, what had brought me here and was that vocation still valid. This was a special time, when I felt that God might be listening to me, hearing my pleas to find my identity, temporal and spiritual. I would sit on a bench in the gardens, or find a quiet spot under a tree, and sit and read, pray and reflect. At these times I felt very much at peace with God and the world, and time and any other concerns (trivial or otherwise) did not matter. These times were very precious, and I still look back on them with huge affection. If I close my eyes, I can still see that young boy sitting under a tree, a book in his lap, at peace with the world, and a sense of being in the right place at the right time.

Although I felt that God heard me at these times, I can't say that I was actually aware of hearing him. However, even in my adolescent mind I did feel that I emerged from these sessions with a greater sense of clarity, and it felt that this was coming from within. I believed that God may be directing my thoughts, if not actually speaking out loud to me. However, although I was happy in this place, it was soon to come to an end and sadly the world will have to wait a bit longer for a Scottish pope.

I left the seminary when I was aged 16, not because of a crisis of faith, nor any feelings that God had rejected me; nor was I dissatisfied with life in the seminary. My departure came after a visit to my father confessor. I was having all the adolescent sexual urges and feeling that God disapproved.

The White Fathers' words, about sin and Hell and damnation, still rang in my ears at these times. In an attempt to help me, my confessor gave me a very graphic description of sex and procreation. He did this by referring to nature, as illustrated by cattle, in particular cows and bulls (to explain, as well as being a priest, he was also the farm manager, and so there was plenty of detail about the mechanics of the act, but there was not a lot of talk about romance and love and tenderness. I'd like to believe that this agriculturally slanted education did not have too much influence on my later approach to women and sex, or my wooing technique.

This meeting disturbed me greatly, and I could not get it out of my mind. Not because of the graphic images of cattle procreating, but I just could not see myself living a life of celibacy. I was already struggling not to sin, in thought word or deed, and was failing on all fronts – frequently! When I talked to my father confessor again, rather than counsel me, and discuss how I might still be able to follow my calling, it was decided that I should leave, as clearly the life of a priest was not for me. It was also decided that there should be no delay and that I should leave the seminary right away, in case I unsettled any of the other boys with my doubts. That was not a personal indictment of me and my ability to influence the college population, it was just the way they tended to handle issues such as doubt. Out of sight out of mind.

I don't remember much about actually leaving the seminary, it was all a bit of a blur as it seemed to be accomplished with indecent haste. However, I do remember a deep sense of failure and futility. Looking back now, my transition back into secular school was not handled very well. Let me qualify that, it was not handled at all! In fairness it happened at a time before the discovery of concepts like emotional intelligence and feelings. Indeed, there was little recognition that someone coming from a deeply immersive experience of an environment where they lived, studied and prayed together 24/7, all with a common purpose and life goal, may actually need a bit of help to decompress and be able to cope with a normal school.

5: Back to School

Returning to my old school was traumatic, a lot more traumatic than anyone at the time realised it was going to be. I don't think I even suspected just how difficult it would be. For my part, I believed the biggest issue was my sense of the loss of my vocation. My hopes of being Pope had been dashed, and I felt that my life was now purposeless. Yes, I know that may seem a bit melodramatic, and that I was taking myself a little bit too seriously. Nevertheless, for many years I had had a certainty about myself and where my life was going. It was clear to me and to my friends and relations – I was going to be a priest – the first priest in our family. Now with that goal gone, I had no further ambition; there was no Plan B. So, while most of my peers were talking about where their future lay, what university they would apply to, what subjects they would study and what career paths they would follow, I could not see any future that appealed to me, nothing really interested me. Nothing felt purposeful, but when your dreams had been to convert entire continents, the prospect of the civil service or working in a bank did not seem very glamorous... my apologies to any civil servants or bank tellers reading this!

Looking back now, one could be forgiven for thinking that this was merely an adolescent, and an immature one at that, being a bit overly dramatic. Of course there was an element of that. However, to dismiss those 'loss' feelings as only that, would be to miss the fact that the John of 1966 was grieving the death of a dream, a role that he had believed would define him, but would now never happen. It was the only career goal that he had ever wanted, and now it was gone for ever. Neither he, nor anyone around him, parents, teachers, friends, the church and especially his schoolmates, understood the depth of that loss. In fairness, it was many years later before I recognised it myself. So, there was no recognition from anyone around him that he needed to mourn that loss, that he needed to come to terms with new life goals, a new secular identity of John as not-priest, and never-pope.

Clearly at that time, with my life certainty gone, there was nothing to replace it, no aim, no ambition. And the careers advice officers who suggested a job in a bank or the civil service were absolutely no help. Indeed, it was to be over two decades before I would find another goal that provided me with some purpose to my life.

Looking back now with that wonderful gift of hindsight, it seems obvious that I John had suffered a huge loss and it seems inconceivable that no one offered help and support. But the times were very different then. Our society was not nearly as emotionally literate as it is now. The then prevailing attitude of a West of Scotland man was, "Sorry about your loss, no use crying over spilt milk, anyway nobody died, so now you just need to man up and get on with life." In hindsight, it is entirely possible that some of the outcomes that the future would bring may have been avoided, if the transition from seminary to secular life had been handled more sensitively. But I don't blame anyone for those outcomes.

I also refute any suggestion that I might have been a victim. It is all too easy in the current climate to claim the badge of victimhood and point the finger at society, my parents, the school, the church and anyone else who may, or may not, have touched my life at that time. But claiming victimhood means relinquishing our agency in our own lives and dilutes our power to change. And I strongly believe in the resilience of human beings, their amazing powers of adaptability to emerge from the ashes of chaos and forge something wonderful and new.

Besides, today I believe that those outcomes, or some version of them, would probably all have happened regardless, even if I had been helped to grieve my loss. All that may have happened is that I would just have less of an excuse for my behaviour. Who knows, certainly not me!

Today I can clearly see that, by leaving the seminary, I was negatively affected in other ways, beyond the loss of a vocation. Another, and perhaps the biggest, issue was that it left me ill-prepared for life in a secular world. I was very shy, and always felt anxious about talking to strangers, or people that I did not know well. It always felt that they were judging me – and the result of the judgement was that they were most definitely finding me wanting. It was never actually clear what it was about me that did not meet their standards; not that I knew what their standards were anyway, I just knew that I was not enough. I was also a bit naïve and found it practically impossible to read people, especially if they were being sarcastic or joking with me. So, I was never really sure how to behave around them. I was so envious of the people who had that apparent casual ease around people, who just knew the right thing to say or to do, who just knew that they were enough, more than enough even – whatever enough was. My theory, only a little bit tongue in cheek, was that there was a big 'Book of Life' that detailed every situation that you would ever meet, and the exact method to handle it, and everyone had read it and then hidden it, so I never got to see it. The result was that socially I often felt like a fish out of water.

Whenever I was in a situation with only one other person, mostly I seemed to be OK. Although often I felt awkward, but sometimes I could be relatively relaxed and even felt fairly safe with the things that I said or shared. But the problems increased as the number of people in the crowd increased. Even if we had all just met, or everyone had known each other for the same amount of time, I was the one who tended to be the outsider, or at least that is the way I felt. Indeed, often in groups I would feel invisible, that nobody really noticed me, or if they did notice me, they did not think that I had anything worthwhile to contribute. So, to stay safe, mostly I didn't contribute very much, but unfortunately this just increased the awkward feelings, the clichéd vicious circle.

I can't put all of these feelings of inadequacy down to leaving the seminary. In the seminary I loved being among lots of boys, it felt like family. Maybe that was because we were all united in our ambition to be priests. Or maybe the spiritual atmosphere of the place affected the relationships between the boys, made it less threatening. Indeed, it was a very benign non-threatening atmosphere. Whatever, I do believe that the sheltered atmosphere of the seminary meant that I was less prepared for the more robust atmosphere of real life as a developing adolescent, than I might otherwise have been. That I was not ready for the cut and thrust of the world where people might be mean to me, or just not like me for arbitrary reasons. However, I also believe that growing up as an only child, meant that I did not have the benefit of siblings that teach us how to interact with others, or compete for attention in a busy, noisy world.

The other kids at the school did not really know what to make of me. Many of them had known me before I went off to the seminary, some of them had even been my friends and classmates before. But this was a different John, and our experiences had diverged greatly. So they tended to see me as this strange person who came across as very prudish and a bit sanctimonious; looking back, they were probably totally justified. For a while, I tried to maintain my spiritual practices and beliefs. I would attend Mass in the morning before school and I would also attend devotions in the evening plus any other services that were happening in our parish church. This set me apart from the other kids, as I was the only one doing it. In fact on weekdays, the only people attending Mass tended to be a couple of older women, the priest and me. After a few weeks of trying to continue my seminary life in a secular environment, I was feeling increasingly isolated.

There was one other boy in my year who had been briefly at the same seminary, and I had known him, although not particularly well. So I thought that he might be an ally for me, or at least someone to share my journey with. However, rather than being a support, he avoided me constantly, and it became increasingly obvious that no one knew anything about this aspect of his past. And obviously he dearly wanted it to stay that way. So he stayed away from me for fear that anyone would discover our connection. I couldn't really blame him, I would have probably done the same.

Unfortunately, I did not have that luxury, as this was the same school that I had attended prior to going to the seminary. So, everyone knew my story. Watching him and the way he interacted with the other pupils and not me, just seemed to highlight my sense of alienation. The big question for me was, how was I going to fit in?

First off, I set out to prove them wrong about their impression of me. I needed to show them that I was not the prudish killjoy that everyone thought that I was. So, I started the post seminary make over, a kind of reverse conversion experience. I learned to swear, even though it didn't sound right to my ear, or to anyone else. It sounded a bit like your poshest, most prissy aunt trying to swear – obviously I needed to practice! Very soon I became one of the smokers in the toilets, and even started underage drinking at weekends. Attendance at morning Mass and devotions decreased and eventually stopped completely. In fact, I avoided going to church whenever possible, as long as my mother wasn't looking that is. I did feel guilty about all of this (it's that word again) but I felt that I needed to behave this way just to survive. Looking back now, I don't think that I ever really felt that I 'fitted in'. Whatever group of people I was with, I always felt that I was never quite comfortable. So, at school I tried to be part of the clever set, while at the same time being part of the cool kids and the rebels. Unfortunately for me, and maybe even for them, I didn't feel very much at home with either group.

Where this inadequacy was at its most obvious was when I was around females. It was difficult for me to talk to females, and the more attractive they were, the worse it got. (OK, I know that is clichéd, and being awkward around attractive girls is part of the job description of being an adolescent boy.) However, during much of my formative adolescent years the only females I had had any dealings with were my mother and nuns. Not exactly a great training ground for flirting and relationship experimentation. So, asking a girl out seemed like a huge risk, which, of course, it usually is. But where for some people, being told 'no' did not seem like a huge deal, for me a rejection felt like something awful, shameful even, where facing a world that knew all about my rejection and humiliation afterwards would be, at best, difficult.

A large part of that reason was that I did not feel comfortable with myself. I did not know who I was any more. I know it's true that many (if not most) adolescents struggle to find their identity. For me, and this is not a self-pity trip (or maybe it is), it was a bit more difficult because I thought that I had my identity all nicely planned out and packaged for the future; then suddenly it was gone and I had to start again building a new one. So, I always felt that I was a couple of years behind my peers, quite immature in many ways. Of course, back then I would not have articulated it in that way. I just knew that I was somehow different and, depending on the day, that could be a good thing or a bad thing! However, what I did not realise was that there was good news coming, the solution was not far away. But more of that later.

I did not enjoy my last couple of years at school, as I was completely devoid of any direction. Most of my classmates (I was still in the top classes) were planning to go to university, but my only ambition was just to be a former pupil. I wanted to leave at the end of fourth year, but my parents insisted that I stay on and get some qualifications. Reluctantly I stayed on, but I became difficult in class, not that I did anything particularly bad, I was just a nuisance and acting the class clown. It was part of my campaign to shed the pious tag and become more accepted. It was not the most successful strategy, either for the other pupils or the staff. Indeed, most of the teachers grew tired of my antics and I was banned from all lessons, somewhat ironically, with the exception of Religious Knowledge which was compulsory. The result was that I left school with hardly any qualifications.

6: First Job

I did leave school with a few friends, especially Paddy, Seamus, Brian, Patricia and Ann Jane and during my late teens we were pretty close, did all the usual things, going to parties, concerts, folk club, pub, etc. We all dated a bit, sometimes got dumped, occasionally got stood up and one of us, Seamus (or Jim as his wife would like him to be called), even got married. I had a long term, if somewhat on and off, girlfriend, Mary Rose. We first met at school and continued to date for about three years.

While most of my classmates went off to university after school, with one O-Level and one Higher, I did not meet the entrance qualifications for any college or university. At the time, this did not bother me, as I had no interest in continuing with my education. All I wanted was to get out and explore what the world had to offer, so I needed to find a job.

Fortunately my dad heard of a vacancy for a data processor with the company where he worked and suggested that I apply, which I did. At first, I was a bit apprehensive as I did not want to be working alongside my dad. On the one hand I was worried that the other workers would be concerned about the nepotism and on the other, I did not want him looking over my shoulder and checking up on me. As it turned out, the company had premises in two different buildings a couple of streets apart. Also, the factory I was to work in was a high security building, and no one could enter without a pass. So to all intents, I could have been working for a completely different company. That reassured me that I would not be under constant scrutiny, well not from my dad at least.

The job required someone to interpret the data that was produced from the destructive testing of thermal batteries. The data came in three forms, a graphic representation, like you might see in an ECG showing the battery output, a digital printout of the voltage second by second and a film of the oscilloscope showing the fluctuation. The batteries were designed to power some functions inside missiles for the military of various NATO countries. So the tests were designed to simulate the conditions that the missiles would experience in flight, and our job was to determine whether or not the batteries would perform within the parameters required, which were pretty exacting. The data processor had to take this data and turn it into an intelligible report for the management to present to the military.

I very quickly learned how to do the various analyses and turned out to be very adept at this job, able to analyse the data both quickly and accurately. So much so that when they needed test results in a hurry, I soon became the go-to person, even though there were others who had been doing the job far longer than I had.

At first I loved being out in the world, working with adults who also treated me as an adult. Much of what was being done there was research, and the specifications for the products were continually changing. Also, the job I had was viewed as a key component of that research. Which gave me some status and meant that I was present at many of the important meetings, and felt part of that team.

It was a bit of a novelty for me, to be recognised as someone who had a valuable contribution to make. In fact it was quite heady brew! Even so, I started to become discontented. The data analysis stopped being a challenge for me, and I found that I needed something more to stimulate me. The test lab that carried out the tests and produced the data was a big attraction for me. All these machines, like enormous vibrators to simulate the turbulence that would be experienced by a rocket in flight, and oscilloscopes with cameras to measure current deviation, they all fascinated me. What they were doing in the lab seemed so much more interesting and exciting than data processing.

I started hanging around the lab and asking questions about what they were doing and why. Fortunately, the guys were happy to show me around some of the equipment and even their own little side projects. It was a time when electronics were becoming popular and many people had hobbies, building things like radio receivers or remote-control model cars. There was a real sense at the time that anything was achievable. It was the 60s, and it was exciting.

Jim, the boss of the test lab, encouraged my interest and suggested that he speak to my boss and arrange to have me transferred to his department. So, I moved to become a member of the test lab team on the condition that I attended day release and gained the entry qualifications to an electronics course. Also, even though I was moving department, the bosses wanted me to make myself available for data analysis, when it was needed. The move from the data processing was not completed immediately. My work schedule meant I had a couple of days in the data processing, a couple of days in the test lab and a day at college. It gave me an interesting and varied time. The data processing office was, apart from me, exclusively female. The test lab was exclusively male. In both of these departments I was, by a good margin, the youngest.

In college, things were different. I was among a mixed group of people my own age, which was a pleasant change. Mostly we were all quite conscientious in attending classes, after all our various employers were paying for our education. However, occasionally a group of us would take an afternoon off. One of the guys' family had a holiday home on Loch Lomond, with a speed boat. So, off we would go, grab some food for a BBQ and sail over to one of the many uninhabited islands on the loch to swim and do a bit of water skiing. These were great days, I was 19 and there was a wonderful sense of fun, freedom and promise.

Despite the opportunity to train in the emerging occupational arena of electronics, I decided that it was time to leave. Many people, in particular my parents, told me that I was mad at throwing away such a great chance. But I just needed to see what lay beyond the limited boundaries of my experience thus far. For that reason, and without much of a plan for the future, I resigned from my job.

Although I was excited for the future, for the great adventure ahead, I was also sad to leave some people who had become such good friends. They were lovely people, who had taken a real interest in the 'baby' of the workplace, and I was going to really miss them. I wonder where they all are now, what happened to them, and dearly hope that that life was kind to them.

7: Mary Rose

A great blessing in my life – I really want to say it – is to have had close relationships with some extraordinary women including a classical pianist, a consultant doctor and a university lecturer. Over the decades I have been engaged to be married four times, married three times and divorced twice. So, although I feel fortunate to have enjoyed the love of these women, the feelings may not be entirely mutual in every case.

The first major relationship I had was with Mary Rose. There had been a few flirtations, some girlfriends that lasted for a few dates, but Mary Rose was the first lasting relationship. We were both in our teens, I was 17 and she a year younger. In total the relationship lasted for around three years. How it began is lost in the mists of time. We had known each other at school, as she had gone out briefly with my friend Brian. Brian was one of these incredibly irritatingly good-looking guys. The type of guy that, when there were girls around and you were standing beside him, you felt invisible. Women (actually girls) loved him and threw themselves at him.

However, he was good to hang around with, if only in the hope that one of the women would bounce off him and land on you.

If my memory serves me well, that's what happened with Mary Rose. For while Brian could attract women with seeming effortless ease, they never tended to stay. Whatever happened, Mary Rose and I started going out and became an item. Mary Rose was a beautiful girl, as my father often pointed out, and she was fun to be around, at least to begin with. This was the 60s (1967 when we met) and things were changing, very quickly. For teens, life seemed so full of endless possibilities. The fashion and the music were exciting, and we were just discovering the effects of alcohol, a whole lot of fun. After a while I wanted to experience some of the other substances that were becoming popular, but living in a small town like Kirkintilloch, this was difficult at best. It would take another couple of decades before the impact of the 60s would reach Kirkie. Indeed, Kirkie's first pub opened in 1968. Kirkintilloch had been a 'dry' town (no pubs) since 1920, which made it the regular butt of music hall jokes, and even inspired a song by the Corries *(There are no pubs in Kirkintilloch)*. The story I was told (and it may even be true) was that after the First World War, before the coal mines were nationalised, they tended to be worked by subcontractors. At the time various subcontractors had a licence to bring in workers who they were responsible for paying. In Kirkie, there were many pubs and many of the contractors were themselves publicans. Payday tended to be a Friday evening and was usually in the pub. So it was no great surprise that many of the men got drunk before going home. Also no surprise that the publicans would allow men credit during the week, as, since they were actually paying their wages, they knew they would get their money back on the Friday. Unfortunately, it was also no surprise that many families received little money for food and rent as much, if not all, of it had been spent in the pub. Therefore, a coalition of the Temperance Movement, the Kirk (Church of Scotland) and the local women petitioned the council, and all of the pubs were closed. Every two years after that, there was a referendum to gauge whether the town wanted to have pubs opened again. Every year the answer was 'no' until 1968, when the Antonine pub opened, Kirkintilloch's first pub in almost 50 years. This event coincided with my friends and I reaching legal drinking age and was precipitated by the influx of Glasgow people, which changed the demographics of Kirkintilloch forever.

My fashion sense (a phrase that many took issue with, suggesting that it may be an oxymoron) was becoming more extreme. I grew my hair long, wore frock coats, beads and tie-dye T-shirts. Mary Rose was a lot staider in her taste but tended to tolerate my experimental approach to haute couture. Her mother was much less tolerant. She was a schoolteacher and her husband was the managing director of a printing firm, roles that she wore like a cloak of status and entitlement. Also they owned their own house, whereas I lived in a council house. Although she was almost too polite to say it out loud, it was obvious who ruled their home, and just as obvious what she thought of her little princess's boyfriend. Indeed her body language needed to be censored. Despite this Mary Rose and I survived as a couple for some years.

At the beginning of 1970, the restlessness that I had been battling really started to boil over. There were big cultural changes happening in the world and I wanted to be part of it all. I wanted to travel. I no longer believed that the world ceased to exist at the Kirkintilloch border. The parochial atmosphere of the town felt suffocating. So, I worked hard at convincing

Mary Rose to come away with me. She was not quite as enthusiastic as I was, in fact I suspected that I might need to kidnap her, especially if she was going to get out of the clutches of the gorgon.

When we discussed it with her mother, she was even less enthusiastic than Mary Rose. Actually 'discussed' is probably the wrong way to describe what happened. Discussed suggests a back and forward of ideas and concepts. That was not quite what happened. We, well I, introduced the subject of going away together. After that there was a lot of backing but very little forwarding. Although there were an awful lot of words used, they all boiled down to ... my daughter ... you ... unmarried... travelling ... no way!!!

So we, well again I, decided that the best way to handle this was to get married. Off I went to the nearest jeweller and returned with an engagement ring. Surprisingly, at least to me, mother did not seem to be too excited that I was intending to make an honest woman of her daughter. She also started throwing, what seemed to me to be rather trivial and irrelevant questions at us, or rather me. Things like where will you get money? What about transport? Where will you sleep? She said these were practical issues, I felt she was just nit-picking.

Undaunted, I started making plans. She was probably right, we needed some transport. So I went to a car auction and saw the perfect vehicle to convert into a camper van. It was a Mercedes hearse! Absolutely perfect! It already had a nice flat rear that could be altered to take a double bed. When I showed it to Mary Rose, she seemed a wee bit doubtful. I can't lie I was a bit disappointed. It appeared that she could not quite grasp my vision.

The real crunch came when I showed it to Mary Rose's mother. If she had previously been a bit unreceptive to our (my) plans, now that I/we had a hearse, her reception of that fact made her previous attitude seem positively effusive. "My daughter is going nowhere in a hearse! Absolutely not, no way!" I have to admire Mary Rose, she did her best to look disappointed. She even tried in a less than half-hearted fashion to persuade her mother to allow her to drive off, as a newly married woman, to a honeymoon that would entail a circumnavigation of the globe in our hearse. Who wouldn't want that? Well, I've since found, a surprisingly large number of people wouldn't and, as it turned out Mary Rose and her mother were two of them.

Disappointed but undeterred, I decided that I was going to go alone. So, after two blissful weeks of engagement, I was back at the jewellers getting most of my money back. Then off to the nearest outdoor shop to buy a rucksack and sleeping bag. Back home, packed some clothes then my father drove me to the motorway where I started hitchhiking to my great adventure. The hearse? Well, the engine exploded when my father tried to reverse it to make space in the car park. Ironically, it had to be taken away on a flatbed truck (a hearse for cars?) and scrapped.

After an emotional farewell accompanied with lots of tears, Mary Rose promised to wait for me forever. We wrote to each other faithfully, or rather she wrote. Then about five months later she arranged to meet me in London. I remember the meeting. We were on the Embankment; it was a dull sort of day. I had had a couple of drinks and saw her coming towards me. She looked really lovely, she always did. She had long hair and a great figure and tended to dress in the style of the times, short dress and long boots. The next bit is a bit vague and, to this day, I'm not entirely sure whether I invented it. What I believe she said was that she was finishing with me, that bit is true, no mistakes there. She was quite clear that she could never be in a relationship with a drug addict. That bit wasn't actually true, well at least not at that time. That she had met someone else, seemingly also true. And that he was in an iron lung, really not sure about that bit! But, if you pardon the bad taste pun, it is a bit deflating to be dumped for someone in an iron lung.

Sadly, that was the last time I ever saw Mary Rose. I thought about her occasionally, and it conjured the surreal picture of her sitting beside a huge metal tube with just a head sticking out the top. However, with us being Kirkie folk, I would get the occasional snippet of gossip about what she was doing. This usually happened when my mother met her parents at Mass on a Sunday morning. Turns out that while the mother disliked me, a lot, and felt that her daughter had had a narrow escape, the father actually liked me and thought that I had 'character'. Maybe that said more about his relationship with his wife than it did about me. Anyway, I did hear that Mary Rose got married and had a couple of children. So he must have got out of the iron lung at least a couple of times. On the other hand, this may have been a strange dream I had. I really don't know. But it did not help my self-esteem to believe that I was dumped for someone in an iron lung.

8: Drop Out

Growing up in a small town can be limiting. For me, growing up in a small town in the 1960s felt almost suffocating. There was so much going on in the world and Kirkintilloch seemed to be quite content, no determined, to stay firmly rooted in the past. True there had been many changes, as the demographics had been altered due to the influx of displaced Glaswegians. But this only seemed to increase the indigenous population's resolve to preserve the old Kirky in a museum ready format, just add labels and cobwebs!

There was a cultural revolution sweeping across much of the world, and I wanted to be part of it. Unfortunately for me Kirky seemed completely insulated from it, like Brigadoon but without the charm. Undaunted, my style in clothes started to reflect that change as I grew my hair, started wearing frock coats, flared trousers and platform shoes, which were really uncomfortable. However, at that time I did not mind suffering for fashion.

My taste in music became increasingly avant-garde and far less mainstream even than my peers. However, Kirky was not exactly a place to discover the latest underground music. The one place that did sell records (yes, actual vinyl) was an electrical shop that sold washing machines, fridges and other household appliances. It also had a record department. When I say 'record department' what I actually mean is that it had a shoebox with a very small selection of music, most of which I would not have been found dead hearing at that time. One day my mother was going shopping so, in a bout of unrealistic optimism, I asked her to bring me back a record – *The Sound of Silence* by Simon and Garfunkel. She tried her best and returned with *The Sound of Silence* by The Bachelors an Irish tenor group who, although I have to admit (from the cushion of a few decades) did a very passable cover of the song, but were very much not cool, which to me as a teenager was so important. She could not understand my disappointment, after all it was the same song. So, she dismissed it as the ingratitude of youth. For me this incident completely encapsulated Kirky's place in the world, a kind of hand-knitted modernism.

There was an exciting world out there, just waiting for me and I needed to get out there and be part of it. Since Mary Rose was not going to come with me, I was going to go by myself. The first stop of my journey of enlightenment to India was to be the Kendal Hotel, in the Lake District. Before leaving Kirkie I had arranged a job in the hotel as a waiter. When I arrived, there was some concern about the length of my hair which meant that I had to wear it in a ponytail for food hygiene reasons. The majority of the clientele comprised of bus tourists in their 60s, so my appearance was considered inappropriate for this group. The result was, my career as a waiter only lasted one meal. After that I worked in the hotel variously as a porter, a dishwasher or a breakfast chef. I enjoyed working in the kitchen, it was the hub of activity for the hotel. Although it could be a bit noisy and tempestuous with a mainland Spanish chef and a Majorcan head waiter, throwing insults and even plates at each other.

What made the Kendal Hotel significant for me was that I met two guys from Middlesbrough, Stewart and Ron. They were travelling to France to pick grapes before journeying on through Europe. Since we found an easy friendship, they asked if I would like to join them and I agreed. So a couple of weeks later, I headed back to Scotland to see my parents and then headed south to meet up with them in Sidmouth, Devon.

As soon as I arrived there, I loved it. There was a group of hippies sleeping on the beach, or in the seafront shelters when it rained, and I immediately felt at home. The pub that most of them drank in was called the Horse and Groom, and that is where I first discovered Scrumpy, a very cheap, but extremely strong cider. First taste is similar to, what I imagine would be, the taste of a concoction designed to descale rusty engine parts. Then the effect kicks in, and you wonder why you have never noticed before that your legs have no bones in them. Rather odd! It is a very cheap way to get drunk and while in Sidmouth, we got drunk a lot.

There was also a lot of drugs around, mostly cannabis, amphetamines and LSD and, again, we felt that it was only polite to join in and be sociable. Well at least Stewart and I did. Ron became increasingly frustrated that we were enjoying the life in Sidmouth far too much and not crossing the channel to France. Eventually he gave up and left us to return home to Middlesbrough.

It was also in the Horse and Groom that I first met Lou. I can still remember the moment, although maybe

I have romanticised and embellished it over the years. It was a lovely evening and the pub was really busy. Sitting on the grass in the pub's beer garden, I noticed this beautiful girl, with very long lustrous brown hair, wearing a full length dress, walk into the bar. She was with a tall, long-haired guy. Both of them sat down on the grass behind me. I was pretty drunk at the time, but I remember telling her how beautiful her hair was, and asked, "Could I touch it?" Incredibly, she said yes, but her companion looked less pleased.

Sitting on the beach the next day, I saw her coming towards me. Flashbacks of the previous evening came rushing back to me, tinged with an excruciating embarrassment, making me want to bury myself in the shingle of the beach. How could I have been so cringeworthy as to ask Lou if I could touch her hair? Please pass by, don't recognise me. But despite my silent pleas, Lou just came over and sat down and started talking to me like an old friend, and that was when we became friends, in that moment and for much of the summer. Although we would become much more to each other later.

In the absence of Ron, Stewart and I continued our wild time of drink, drugs and women. To earn a bit of money, I took a job at the local five-star hotel as a dish washer, a job that we colourfully called 'pearl diving', sounded better, more romantic. One morning after a wild night, the manager arrived at the door to find Stewart and myself in bed with two girls. As the only employee, I was sacked on the spot while the others were banned from the hotel. One of the girls was Maggie, a friend of Lou's and someone who was to figure in my life again, in the not-too-distant future.

A couple of weeks after Ron departed, Stewart and I decided that we would take a trip up to London and buy cannabis to bring back and sell. It would keep us supplied with drugs and we would maybe make a little money, by selling some to the other hippies as well. There was also a big concert on at Hyde Park with John Sebastian, Canned Heat and Eric Burdon with War, and we wanted to go to it. At the time Marble Arch was being cleaned, so it was boarded up. By prising a couple of boards aside we could get inside and have a cosy night at one of the most prestigious addresses in London. OK, so the room service was not great, but you can't have everything.

The next day we met up with a couple of Hell's Angels who took us back to their place where we bought some cannabis to take back to Sidmouth and sell to the other hippies. At least that was the plan. What really happened was that, since we as hitchhikers were permanently stoned, we just accepted lifts wherever they were going. Eventually, after a convoluted journey back from London, we found ourselves in the New Forest with a load of cannabis. Naturally we did what most self-respecting hippies would do in the circumstances, we smoked a lot of dope and wandered around the forest indulging in an orgy of tree hugging. We also smoked a lot of the cannabis we were going to sell, then arrived back in Sidmouth only to find most of the hippies had gone. Some of them had gone to the festival on the Isle of Wight while other part-time hippies had gone back home, to return to university and college. So our foray into drug entrepreneurship ended with very little product left and no customers either. Pablo Escobar was probably breathing a sigh of relief that we would not be taking over his drug empire just yet.

A couple of days later we took a trip to Exeter with a couple of girls who were working in one of the local hotels. In one of the pubs we got our ears pierced with a needle and a matchbox. Seemed like a good idea at the time, and the more scrumpy I drank, the better the idea seemed. Then we wandered round some shops, where I later discovered, Stewart was indulging in a bit of shoplifting. He had not stolen anything of any value, just a couple of passport wallets and some little trinkets. When we got back to Sidmouth, Stewart went off to spend the night in one of the girls' room. The one I was with, who was a bit older, would not let me into her room, so off I went to the beach, feeling rejected and sorry for myself.

The next day Stewart's girl came and found me on the beach. She then told me that the police had raided the hotel during the night and Stewart had been arrested. I went off to the local police station to see what I could find out, and hopefully get Stewart out of jail. It turned out he had been charged with possessing stolen goods, possession of drugs and statutory rape. This is when we discovered that the girl he was with, although she looked much older, was in fact only 15 years old. I put on my best 'I know my rights' face and asked to see Stewart, but the police were extremely unimpressed and refused. Instead they told me that if I did not leave town that day, I would also be arrested and charged. Sadly, I never did see Stewart again, so I have no idea what happened to him.

It was a few days before I took the police's 'advice' and left town. I went off with another friend, Declan from Ireland. We had no real plan about where we should go. Declan said he knew a girl who was a student at Birmingham University, so maybe we should head north. Since I had no plan whatsoever, even this tenuous one seemed like a good idea to me. Besides, I had received a letter from Maggie who said that, should I come to Birmingham, she would like to see me, that she had something she wanted to talk to me about. Declan thought that this sounded rather ominous.

After a couple of days hitching lifts and sleeping in fields, we finally arrived in Birmingham and Declan managed to contact his friend. She met us and then sent us to another friend of hers in Moseley Village, a district of Birmingham where I ended up staying for a few months in a flat. The term we used to describe this and other flats like it was 'crash pad', which was basically somewhere one could find a place to sleep for a night or longer. Notice I did not say you could find a bed, it was usually a bit of floor where you could spread out. That particular flat became, an informal commune over the next few months. The owner of the flat – or rather the person whose name was on the rent book – was Caroline. She was a bit of a *prima donna* who liked to control everything that happened, from the comfort of her bed. It was a strange place, with an odd mix of people and a lot, really a lot, of drugs. You could get just about anything that you wanted, from cannabis to heroin and everything in between. Declan left after a week or so and returned to Dublin, but I stayed on there for a few months over the winter.

I did go to meet up with Maggie, and it turned out, as Declan suspected, that she was pregnant. She said that she wanted us to get married, so that we could bring up the baby together. But I could not see that happening. We had not spent more than a couple of nights together. So we hardly knew each other and, besides, I was not in love with her. So, I felt that marriage was almost certainly a recipe for disaster. My lifestyle was not what anyone would mistake for someone who was good, or even mediocre, marriage material. Nevertheless, she insisted that I went home with her to meet her parents. Maybe she thought that they would persuade me to make an honest woman of her. With raging guilt shouting down my better judgement, I agreed. One consolation to me was that Maggie's mother most definitely agreed with me about whether I represented a good catch. In fact she made her opinion crystal clear and at great length, and with quite considerable volume, on the off chance that I failed to grasp her meaning. After rejecting any suggestion of a union between me and her precious daughter, her parents, well really her mother, told me to get out of her house and never under any circumstances should I see her daughter ever again. So I did as ordered and left, thinking that this was the end of the episode.

Maggie left home soon after. The atmosphere in the house had become toxic between her mother and her, so she moved to a little flat of her own. Unfortunately, she had a fall one day and lost the baby. It is one of the episodes in my life that I still feel guilty when I think of it. Nevertheless, I am still certain that marriage would have been a disaster and, in view of how my life was to turn out later, she had a very lucky escape. However, as fate would have it, this was not the last time I was to see Maggie, as she popped up again in extremely bizarre circumstances. But that was to come later.

Life in Moseley Village became a round of drink, drugs and sex. The drug scene got heavier, as more opiates and amphetamines became available. Even a couple of fatalities did little to stop the drug abuse that seemed rampant in the community. I mostly avoided the opiates, but I was using cannabis and LSD very heavily and it was at this time that I was to have my first 'bad trip'.

I was in bed with my girlfriend and we had taken some LSD, so we were both tripping. Then one of the housemates, a Hell's Angel who also suffered from schizophrenia, started to get violent and ranting and throwing things around the house. These are not good circumstances to be tripping in. So we quickly got out of the house and went to a friend's flat nearby. But the damage had been done. Visibly upset, my girlfriend was struggling not to descend into a panic attack. It was probably my attempts at trying to look after her that helped me to keep it together. Eventually the drug wore off and we were left physically and emotionally drained. But the incident left a scar: whenever I got anxious, I would have flashbacks to that night and the bad feelings.

After a few months I became close friends with a guy called Paul, who was born and bred in Birmingham and lived nearby with his parents. He wanted to move out of his parents' house and I needed to get out of Caroline's house. So together we found a bedsit and moved in and shared the rent. It was a rather crazy flat. We had found an old, abandoned hostel and had salvaged some mattresses, which we spread all over the floor. The flat had an open-door policy, so all comers were welcome, and if you brought drugs, you were absolutely welcome! We never knew from one day to the next who, or even how many, would be staying in this tiny flat. The local chapter of the White Panthers, a revolutionary anti-establishment group, often had meetings in our flat. And since the leader was one of the biggest drug dealers locally, they 'paid rent' by leaving us some cannabis. So, of course, we encouraged this civic use of our premises. It felt very public spirited of us.

I also had another foray into the drug dealing business. Every dole day, Paul and I would take our money and buy cannabis from my White Panther pal. We would then divide it up into deals (parcels to sell) and sell it down the pub. This meant that we could at least double our money every week and that gave us drugs for ourselves, money to drink and even some money for food. It seemed very entrepreneurial of us.

Come the early summer, it was time to journey south again. My plan was to return to Sidmouth and just see what was going on and then take things as they came. However, before doing that I wanted to visit the *Divine Light Mission,* an ashram in the middle of Golders Green. My interest in spiritual matters had risen to the surface again and I had started reading some alternative theological texts such as *The Book of Mormon* and some of the eastern holy books such as the *Bhagavad Gita* or *The Tibetan Book of the Dead.*

I felt that I needed to find meaning for my life, as I was just drifting, geographically and spiritually. Some of my reading had led me to discover a young 13-year-old teacher, Guru Maharaj Ji. The rumours were that he was the incarnation of God, and, somewhat strangely, he was currently living in the ashram in Golders Green. So, I wanted to visit and see for myself what he was all about. I managed to get admitted to the ashram and stayed there for a couple of weeks. The setup in the ashram was very loose: on most days the guru would teach for about an hour or so talking about peace and enlightenment. It all seemed very noble, and very much in keeping with the zeitgeist of that time. But I can't say that it really touched me in any particularly deep way. But that could be down to a lack of commitment and my 'extra-curricular' activities while I was there.

The house next door had a cannabis farm in the attic. For that time, this was quite a substantial farm. I quite quickly made friends with the owners and most days I would climb over the wall between the ashram and the cannabis farm and join my new-found friends for a chat over tea and joints. This made for a very interesting time, where every day I was high, either through meditation and spiritual teaching, or through this organic cannabis; sometimes it was both. Then we heard that Guru Maharaj Ji was going to appear at a new music festival that was going to take place in Glastonbury. So I decided that I would make my way to this festival. This was only the second festival at Glastonbury, and it was a much smaller, more intimate affair than it is today. The people at the festival tended to be people like myself, hippies and travellers. There were no caravans or enormous tents that looked like canvas houses. I had no idea at the time that this was going to turn into the corporate phenomenon that is Glastonbury today. But then nobody did.

I think I enjoyed the festival. It is all a bit of a blur with memory fragments here and there. One thing I do remember is dancing naked in a cornfield behind the main stage as Traffic played. But I have no idea why? Well I kind of do know why. There were copious amounts of drugs and all these generous people just kept offering them to me, so, being a sociable and polite sort of chap, I just took them. Two weeks later I was still at the festival site, as I had stayed on to help them clear the place up. This was an enjoyable period, it was a simple sort of time, friendly and purposeful. I would probably have stayed longer, but the group started to break up. So, it was back to my original plan and head for Sidmouth again.

When I got there, the atmosphere had changed considerably from the previous year. Firstly, there were fewer hippies around than the previous year, and the town seemed generally much quieter. Later I found out that the locals had turned against the hippies, or the hairies as they called them. Lots of shops had signs on the door – No Hairies – and the police were threatening to prosecute anyone they found sleeping rough.

So what had happened? There were probably many reasons, but there seemed to be three main ones for this change in attitude. First, many of the local girls, and some more mature ladies who had trouble remembering girlhood, found the hippies attractive. There was a romance surrounding the free, vagabond lifestyle that appealed to them. However, many of the parents did not see, or maybe they saw all too clearly, the attraction and voiced their moral outrage about these drug-taking layabouts. They were adamant that they did not want their daughters, or any other member of their household, to associate with such bad influences.

Second, some of the local shopkeepers were losing money, as some of the hippies 'liberated' some of their goods. Although this 'liberation' was presented as ostensibly an ideological commentary on the tension between Capitalism versus Marxism and helping to further the cause of the redistribution of wealth. In reality it was just slang, and justification, for shop lifting.

The final nail in the coffin had been driven in the previous year by two part time hippies from the Midlands, who saw themselves as revolutionaries. As a reprisal for the editor of the Sidmouth Herald writing a rather disparaging opinion piece about the hippies, they had posted a petrol bomb through the letterbox of the paper's office. Fortunately, they carried out their attack in the evening, after the pub closed, so there were no casualties, but there was a fair bit of damage to the office.

Afterwards, the perpetrators expected to be feted as heroes who had struck a righteous blow against 'the man' in the cause of freedom. Instead, most of the hippies, including me, regarded them as immature idiots and wanted nothing to do with them or their actions. So strong was the disapproval from the group that 'our heroes' decided to go back home and, as far as I know, they never returned to Sidmouth again.

The fact that, apart from these idiots, the hippies were unanimous in their condemnation of the firebomb, or any other violent acts, was of little consequence. The hippies were regarded as being collectively responsible and demands were made on the local council and the police to do something about it. So doors were fixed to the seafront shelters, and they were locked at night while the police would carry out a sweep of the beach and local area to ensure that no one was sleeping rough. This was the landscape that met me when I arrived back in Sidmouth. I had been excited and looking forward to coming back, as although my previous visit had ended on a low note, I had some very good memories of Sidmouth. I had met some people that I really liked. And I very much enjoyed the barbecues on the beach, sometimes with fish that we had caught that day. There were a couple of decent musicians among the group, and we would sing along to Bob Dylan, Roy Harper and Simon and Garfunkel songs, as the sun went down. If it had been a warm day, some of us would swim in the sea. For me, it had been a happy time.

However, it was a very different atmosphere from the previous year that greeted me and there were very few faces that I recognised, mostly just locals. Nevertheless, despite or maybe because of, these changes, this year would have a greater impact on my life than even the previous one did.

9: Jesus Loves

Sidmouth was a very different place than it had been the previous year. So was I. After a steady diet of hallucinogenic drugs and eastern mysticism, my mind was in a very fragile state. Looking back now I am convinced that I was very close to a mental breakdown. At the time booze, in particular scrumpy cider, seemed to help keep me sane. Although, knowing what I know now, I'm certain that was an illusion, and the booze was in fact exacerbating the issue. I do remember having quite disturbing flashbacks from the LSD. For example I was in the London Inn, a pub in Sidmouth, and suddenly everyone in the bar looked like they were two-dimensional cardboard cut outs of themselves. This scared me, and I had to get out of there before I had a full-blown panic attack. Unfortunately, this kind of thing was happening increasingly regularly, and it was getting more difficult to control.

Coupled with the aftermath of drug abuse, the hostile atmosphere in Sidmouth was not helping my mental state. Having to play hide and seek every night, just to find somewhere to sleep that the police would not find me, just added to the stress. On reflection, I don't know why I did not just move on to somewhere else. But fortunately I didn't. Who knows where I would be today if I had. What I do know is that this book would definitely have been very different if I had.

After a couple of nights playing 'dodge the cops' as I tried to find a place to sleep for the night, rescue came. It came in the shape of a little grey minivan with a couple of long-haired occupants and my rescuer – Lou.

At the time Lou was associated with a bunch of Christians who lived in a large house in the nearby village of Sidbury. It seemed there was a mini revival happening in the area, and many of the hippies were becoming Christians. Apparently this was part of the wider Jesus movement which saw many hippies joining together in Christian communes such as the Children of God. A couple who were house sitting for the owners of a large house in Sidbury, had opened up the house to some of these converts. The result was an ad hoc commune with a very fluid membership, as new people joined and others moved on.

On the night that they found me, they had been driving around and had found me wandering the streets looking for somewhere to sleep. Since Lou recognised me, they stopped and, after a brief conversation, they offered me a bed for the night. I obviously jumped at the offer, at least this was one night that I did not need to worry about being awoken in the middle of the night by the police.

I was extremely grateful to have the opportunity of a safe place to sleep for a night and so I did not ask any questions. Therefore, I was not expecting the subsequent ambush. When we got back to the house, almost immediately they started into trying to convince me that I should give my life over to Jesus. Since over the years I had become increasingly disillusioned by religion, of all sorts, I was having none of it. As I said earlier, at the time alcohol and drugs were taking a real toll on me mentally and physically. I had lost a lot of weight, and I was having flashbacks and panic attacks. In fact, I was really a bit of a mess when Lou and the others found me, and they felt that they could save me.

In fact they considered it their duty to preach the gospel at me. After what turned out to be a night of evangelistic sparring, I was still adamant that I was not going to be taken in by these happy-clappy Christians with their psychedelic 'Jesus Loves' stickers on their lapels. In the morning Lou's dad (who was a local pastor) came to the house and Lou asked if I would have a word with him. I couldn't see any problem talking to him, he was certainly not going to convince me any more than the others had.

We wandered down to the bottom of the garden where, rather coincidentally, and perhaps symbolically, there was a small orchard of apple trees. To this day I have no idea what he said, or even if he said anything. All I know is that suddenly the world seemed to be very bright, blindingly so. Then I was down on my knees holding onto this man's legs and sobbing like a baby as something broke inside me. The sobbing came not from distress or pain, but from a wonderful release of emotion. The fear and constant dread that I had lived with for months were gone, and instead the feelings I had were a mixture of elation and peace.

I had experienced this kind of peace before. During my retreats in the seminary I had felt this way, a feeling of being in the right place at the right time. That I did not need to go anywhere else, just relax and enjoy the moment. It felt like it had been a long time since I had experienced such peace in my soul.

We lived in that house for an idyllic summer. Our little commune became very close, and we really tried to live by Christian principles, praying together, learning about the Bible and our God and living by faith. God was good and turned up with gifts such as pasties and bread rolls. To many people that probably sounds ridiculous, but some mornings we would find a box on the doorstep with food and provisions and, amazingly, it always seemed to be the correct amount for the household. No one knew then where they came from, and to this day we still don't know. As I said, the numbers in the commune were very fluid and people came and went, but if pasties were delivered, it was always the right number. Maybe there is a pasty angel for these sorts of contingencies, maybe it's a celestial Deliveroo!

We had very little income, so we tried to enhance it by making bird boxes, which was not a great success. It's a huge amount of time-consuming work to make one little bird box for very little reward. I also took some casual work, digging ditches at a local building site and labouring for a road gang, who were building the infrastructure for a small housing estate. It was hard physical work, something that I was not used to. However, I was young and fairly fit and motivated to bring some extra income into the house. So it was not too bad.

Lou and I became a couple during that summer. Sometimes she would stay the night at the Sidbury house, and other times she would go home to her parents' house in Sidmouth. One night she asked me if I would like to come back with her and stay at her parents' house. That night after her parents had gone to bed, we started kissing and telling each other how much we liked each other. From that night we were a couple.

Lou's friend Linda received word that Maggie was coming to visit us in Sidbury. To avoid any awkwardness, Lou suggested that we keep our relationship secret. This seemed like a sensible idea, as I had not seen or had any contact with Maggie since the disastrous meeting with her parents in Birmingham. Unsurprisingly, I was a bit nervous about meeting her again, and how she would feel and act towards me. While my life had not exactly always been straightforward or conventional up to that point, this turned out to be the start of a very strange episode indeed.

Maggie duly arrived with some guy. (After all these years I can't remember his name, so I'll refer to him as Gerry.) At the time we were unsure about his relationship with Maggie, whether he was a friend, or something more intimate. She seemed friendly enough towards me, and there was no sense of resentment or anger regarding our previous encounters. In a rather matter of fact way, she told me about the deterioration of her relationship with her mother, having to leave home and the loss of the baby. Nevertheless, there was an understandably uncomfortable atmosphere between us. So, although we did not actually avoid each other, we did not make a point of seeking each other's company either.

Gerry was a very strange person. Physically he was not particularly remarkable. He was quite stockily built, although not very tall, dark hair and wore sunglasses constantly indoors and outdoors. I don't usually talk about someone's aura, it all sounds a bit new age, but with him, it was difficult to ignore. He did not really engage in conversation, mostly he was 'just there' and there was an air of malevolence and menace about him. At first, I thought that I was just imagining it, that my guilty conscience regarding Maggie was making me perceive things. Certainly, every time that Maggie and

I were together having a conversation, it felt that his eyes were boring into me. It felt very creepy. Later I was to learn that I should trust my instincts.

During their stay at Sidbury we, the commune that is, went to a Christian gathering at a large house in the country. It was hosted by some mature Christians and was well attended by many others from local evangelical churches. During this gathering I was approached by the host and another man who asked me to accompany them to a room at the back of the house. When I arrived, there was around a dozen people in the room, including Maggie. One of the men, who seemed to be the leader, asked Maggie and myself to come together in front of him. I can't remember his exact words, but the gist was that they had sensed a 'spirit' between Maggie and me. That this was a very destructive spirit, and they were going to perform an exorcism on us to cast it out. Well, tea, scones and exorcism were not exactly the combo I had been expecting for a day in the country, not even in Devon!

I have no idea who, if anyone, had told them about our prior history, or whether they had spiritually discerned the connection. Or–I had trouble with this possibility–we really did have some malevolent spirit squatting in our psyches that was obvious to these devout Christians but not to us. Whatever the reason, we knelt in front of this group who encircled us and laid hands on us and prayed fervently and loudly for our release. At the end, everybody smiled at us and hands were shaken, and hugs were given. All in all, everyone seemed satisfied that good work had been done.

I don't know how Maggie felt after this intervention, but I felt a little bit disappointed and bemused. The whole episode had been rather underwhelming to me. Maybe it was naïve of me, but I expected a bit more drama from an exorcism. You know the sort of thing, a manifestation of some spectral being, à la *Ghostbusters*. The only drama was the facial expressions and sonority of the leader's voice – very Old Testament, prophetesque even. As for me I felt a sense of bemusement, being unsure how I had allowed this to happen at all, although the reality was that no one had asked for my permission. The group were obviously well-meaning and convinced of the righteousness of their intervention. They may even have been correct in their assumptions, but I don't remember anyone asking us what we thought, whether this was something that we felt might be beneficial. Other than these feelings, I did not feel any different post exorcism than I had before.

A couple of days after the exorcism event, I was again sleeping the night at Lou's parents' house, in a deep slumber on the floor in her father's study, when suddenly I woke up feeling terrified. It was not like waking up from a nightmare, rather it was more like wakening into a nightmare. The whole of the study seemed to be dripping in malignancy. I had experienced a lot of bad trips and flashbacks over the years, and, although at the time I assumed that this was yet another flashback, even though it had a different, much more sinister feel. Bad trips and flashbacks tended to be centred inside your head, but this felt external. I cowered there in my sleeping bag for much of the night, and was so glad to see the light of the morning.

The next day I was back at the Sidbury house and chatting to another commune member, my fellow countryman Ross, and I told him about my terrifying night. I expected him to dismiss the incident as part of the damage that I had done to myself through my substance use. Instead, he looked very serious and said that was a 'sending'. This meant absolutely nothing to me, I'd never heard of a sending. He explained that Gerry had confided in him that he was a high-ranking warlock, and he had told Ross that he was going to hurt me because of my involvement with Maggie. He said that he was in love with Maggie and saw my presence as a threat to him having a relationship with her. His method of hurting me was this 'sending', which is basically something like a waking nightmare.

My reaction to Ross' revelation was to laugh, although admittedly it was a rather mirthless and unconvincing laugh. The terror feelings of the night before were all too recent for me to completely dismiss this as a joke. Ross then told me that he had dabbled in black magic himself, and he was convinced that Gerry was the real deal. Certainly, he had a very uneasy presence, and the atmosphere tended to change if he walked in a room, and most certainly not for the better. I decided that it would be wise to avoid him till he left.

A couple of days later, I returned to the house to find everyone in a high state of excitement. Both Ross and Dai (the house sitter) were looking rather dishevelled. The story they told was, that Gerry had come into the house and basically just freaked out. The presence of Christian pictures, symbols and books had seemed to have a strong adverse effect on him. He had started shouting and screaming and throwing things around the room. When anyone tried to calm him, it just seemed to make him worse. Finally, he ran screaming from the house.

Dai and Ross pursued him and eventually cornered him in the village. Gerry then attacked them, and they had huge difficulty trying to subdue him. Later, Dai made the observation that Ross was six foot three and had once been a pub bouncer, while Dai although not as tall, was not small either and had been a soldier till recently. Even so they only just managed to subdue Gerry. They said that it was a very frightening incident, as he was frothing at the mouth and tossing them about like rag dolls. They could neither persuade nor force him to return to the house, and finally Gerry broke free and ran off.

Later that day we heard that Maggie and Gerry had packed up and gone, presumably back to Birmingham. There was a collective sigh of relief in the house as we tried to return to our customary calm and peaceful existence.

However, that was not the end of the story. A couple of weeks later we got news of the disturbing postscript to this story. It was no great revelation to us that Gerry had romantic intentions towards Maggie. However, it was also just as clear that Maggie did not view him in that way. After the trauma of the past year, the split with her mother and losing the baby, she wanted and needed a friend that she could depend on for support. When she had explained her need to Gerry and suggested that they should not see each other again, Gerry had exploded. He kidnapped Maggie, as he seemed to think that, given time with him, she would come to view him romantically (presumably the Stockholm Syndrome approach to wooing). The police then became involved and the whole scene developed into a hostage situation. Finally, Maggie was released and returned to her family home and Gerry ended up in Broadmoor, the secure hospital for the criminally insane. That was the last I saw or heard of either Gerry or Maggie.

After they left, we returned to normal, and life continued on its merry way in Sidbury. However, there was one big event to come and even the local press attended and reported on the 'hairies' in a favourable light for a change. Lou's dad, the one who whose knees I cried on, was the pastor to one of the local Churches, Emmanuel. He was having a baptism ceremony at the church and agreed to baptise all the new Christians in our little community.

It was a great occasion, very joyous. There were about eight of us baptised. Someone found me a pair of white trousers and a white shirt, so I looked very saintly. I had been baptised as a baby, as most Catholic babies are, so obviously I don't remember anything about that time. But that was just a little bit of water over the head, this was a full immersion job. We had to give our testimony prior to being baptised. I remember talking about my use of alcohol and drugs and, although most of the congregation were very supportive, two little old ladies disapproved and walked out. Years later someone, who I had not known at the time, but who had actually been baptised that with us that day, gave me a clipping from the paper about the event. In it they quoted me as recanting my life of drugs. Which, at least at that time, was true.

At the end of the summer Lou returned to the Royal College of Music in London. Shortly afterwards, the First Festival of Light took place with a march through London and a rally in Trafalgar Square. Lou and I joined this march with some other friends and thousands of Christians from all over the country. At the end of the rally I made a beeline for the station to take a train to Poole. I had decided that God was calling me to attend the Bible College in Poole. When I got down there, I managed to get an interview. They listened to me very respectfully, but at the end turned me down. Their reason was that I had only been a Christian for a couple of months. If I would like to apply again in two years, they would be glad to see me. But, at this time...

With Lou being at the Royal College of Music, I decided to move to London. I got a job as a driver, delivering and installing jukeboxes and fruit machines round the London area. Not the best job in the world but it had its perks. One of them was that I could take the van home at night, giving me transport, and the other was that I got to know the London streets quite well.

Then one day, what seemed to me to be out of the blue, Lou suggested that we should stop seeing each other and without even asking why, I said, "Well, if that is what you want, then fine." Childishly, I would not let her think that it mattered to me. As I saw it, I had maintained my pride and my dignity. This seemed to surprise Lou as she said that she had expected me to make a scene or at least react. Instead, I just said goodbye and walked out the house. As soon as I was round the corner and out of sight, I allowed myself to cry bitterly against a wall. I did not want the relationship to end, but my pride would not allow her to think that I was dependent on her. Thinking about it now, this was not my most mature moment but, for some reason, I would not, could not, allow her or anyone else to see that I cared more for them than they did for me.

A short while after the breakup I decided to return to Scotland for a short break, to lick my wounds before heading off on my travels again. I found a live church in Glasgow much to my mother's disapproval. She could not understand why I would not go back to the Catholic church of my youth, instead of this 'Protestant church'. I attended the Glasgow church a couple of times and, although I did enjoy being there, it felt like something was missing. I was not sure what it was, but I never really felt a part of it. Maybe I was just missing the friends that I had made in Devon. One Sunday, as I was heading towards the church, I met some old friends. They were heading to the pub and had some cannabis for later; did I want to come with them? After the briefest of struggles, I joined them and never attended that church again.

As an observer it would be easy to dismiss my earlier conversion as merely a way of trying to impress a girl, that there was no real substance to it. The speed of my return to booze and drugs would seem to lend weight to such a suggestion. However, at the time and even now with the benefit of hindsight, I truly believe that interpretation of my fall from grace would be wrong.

My experience in the Sidbury garden and the many other 'God encounters' I had during that time were genuine. And there no way that I can deny them or dismiss them as a mating ploy. True, it is difficult to understand my fall from grace and the speed with which it happened. The only explanation that I can offer for being so fickle is this: my addiction was working in me, long before anyone would have diagnosed it.

10: Sandra

Shortly after my return to Scotland my father was diagnosed with cancer and my parents needed me to be around. So my planned short stay at home had to be extended and, apart from holiday time, I never went travelling again. Instead I got a job in the local psychiatric hospital and trained as a psychiatric nurse. The next twelve years spanned a dark time in my life. It was not so much what was happening around me, as what was happening within me. I was broken. I had no ambition and had not had any since I had left the seminary and my prospects of being a priest had vanished. I had turned away from the Christianity that I had found so comforting in Devon and returned to my old ways and old haunts. During this period I had very little volition or drive. Life just seemed to happen to me; I drifted in and out of relationships, a couple of married women, a few weekend hippies, some nurses and just about any female who wanted me. My drinking and drug use had increased again and, although I would have denied that it was out of control, it was definitely escalating.

It was at this time that I met Sandra, my first wife and the recipient of my worst excesses of drug taking, drinking and selfish behaviour. Looking back now, it is clear that she got all of the bad bits of me and very little of the good. Something that I'm sad about, as she was a sweet and gentle soul.

I first met her in the Byre, which was a very popular pub in Glasgow. Back in the early 70s the Byre was a great hangout for hippy types who liked to listen to rock music and wanted to buy drugs. Both were in abundant supply there, which was why, on a weekend especially, the place was usually packed out. At weekends, there were even queues outside of people waiting to get in.

I can't remember how we met, I think someone in our crowd knew her or her friends and brought her into the company one night. I liked her immediately, she was quite petite, very neat figure, pretty face and a nice casual sense of style. I remember she was wearing an off white rather rustic looking woollen jacket which she told me she had brought back from Greece, where she had been working for a year as a nanny. This little bit of her history set her apart from most of the people in the pub, most of whom had never been anywhere, except maybe on holiday. My friends and I were having a party, well actually we were having our usual weekend open house where anyone with some booze and/or some cannabis, or any other substances, were welcome. These gatherings were usually alcohol and drug fuelled crazed behaviour and sometimes, if we were really lucky, also involved sex.

I'm not sure how Sandra felt about her introduction to this bacchanalia, and, if I'm honest, I don't think

I bothered to ask her. Our group just tended to take it for granted that everyone would enjoy this kind of gathering. In fairness, the majority of the people that comprised our crowd did tend to enjoy it, otherwise what were you doing there. What I do know is that, after we were married, Sandra banned this group from our house after only one party, and she was always reluctant to meet up with them. So, I suppose that tells us something about how she felt about them.

Although she was not a big believer herself, Sandra's heritage was very Catholic. Her mother, Peggy, was an Irish Catholic and her father, who died before I met her, had been an Italian Catholic. Her father came from a fairly wealthy family that had once owned a number of cafés in Glasgow and had made a very good living. Unfortunately, Sandra's grandfather had been a gambler and had lost most of the family's fortune. So, Sandra had grown up on a council estate, same as I had.

We quite quickly became a couple and, while she was much more reserved than the rest of my friendship group, she seemed happy enough being with us. So our relationship grew stronger, and Sandra started talking about making it permanent. I was less sure at that time, I was having a good time and felt that I was only 24 – far too young to settle down.

One night we were going to a party and on the way in I met an old girlfriend, Maureen. She was a beautiful, statuesque girl who smoked and drank pints like a man. My relationship with her had not involved much in the way of small talk. Instead it had been the kind of passionate affair where we almost always got drunk, smoked lots of cannabis and literally ripped each other's clothes off. I had not seen her for some time and so I asked Sandra to go on into the party without me, that I would join her in a couple of minutes. I just wanted to catch up with Maureen, but she had different ideas and almost immediately we could not keep our hands off each other.

I'm ashamed to say that I ran into the party, told Sandra that our relationship was finished. Ironically, I think that at the back of my mind, I felt I was being a gentleman by informing her in person like that. I then went back to Maureen and we raced off to her flat and started another frenzied relationship. I'm not sure how long it lasted, not that long. However, I do remember vividly how it finished. We were living together in her flat and I came home from working nights to find her in bed with another ex-boyfriend. When I walked in, they looked a bit worried about what I was going to do, was I going to get violent, scream and shout? Instead, I just looked at them, said goodbye and walked out never to return. It was ironic that the relationship ended just as it began, with infidelity. Perhaps it was inevitable that it ended that way. Although I was angry and felt betrayed, at the same time I felt that the relationship between us had been all fireworks and no depth, and at that time I felt that I needed more, I needed some depth and stability, not too much though, just a little bit.

Sandra and I did get back together, much to the disgust of her mother. We met in the Byre again and after a grovelling apology, she forgave me. In fact, soon afterwards we got married. I was not really involved in the plans for the wedding. That fell mostly to Sandra and her mother, well mostly her mother. She insisted that it had to be a big Catholic wedding in the local chapel, with an equally big reception in a very exclusive and very grand Catholic club. Peggy's brother was a member of this club, and so we got permission to have our reception there.

I was instructed that it would be expected (expected seems too weak a term) that I take communion at the

Wedding Mass. Therefore, I had to go to confession the night prior to the wedding. At that time, I was not a practising Catholic, had not been for a few years. In fact I barely believed in God anymore, as I considered myself to be an agnostic. When it came my turn to confess, I went off into the confessional and started in the usual manner "Bless me Father for I have sinned, it has been a few years since my last confession". Then I said to the priest. "I have a bit of dilemma, I'm getting married tomorrow and I need to take communion, is it OK to do that if I don't believe in the Catholic church?"

It sounded like the priest was choking on the other side of the grill. The next day it was the same priest who performed the wedding ceremony and, although I may have imagined it, I'm sure that he stared at me in a hostile manner through the whole service. But of course, since the secrecy of the confessional is sacred, he could not say anything to me or anyone else.

The wedding went well, everyone seemed to enjoy themselves. Not quite everyone: towards the end of the reception, Peggy my new mother-in-law, sought me out and started shouting at me, something about a ring and Iain, my best man. Eventually I managed to get her to calm down enough to tell me why she was so upset. It appeared that she had given Iain her engagement ring for safekeeping, and he seemed to have lost it. Why she had taken her ring off, and why she had given it to Iain, was a bit of a mystery; how Iain had managed to lose it was an even bigger mystery. She, of course, accused Iain of stealing her ring, but despite his strenuous denials, he could not offer any explanation about what happened to the ring.

From that day onwards Peggy regarded Iain as a thief and me as an accomplice by association. She seemed to regard the wedding as an elaborate plan on my part to stage a diamond heist to relieve her of her valuables. Indeed, she would bring the subject up for years to come. Personally, I don't believe that Iain stole Peggy's ring, he may have been a bit unreliable, make that totally unreliable, but he was honest. I would trust him not to steal my valuables, I just wouldn't trust him to look after them.

After the reception Sandra and I went on honeymoon. We had nothing planned, so we took a taxi to the main bus station in Glasgow and decided to take the first bus which was leaving, regardless of destination. As it turned out this game of honeymoon roulette took us to Inveraray, a lovely little town sitting on the shore of Loch Fyne. It was a beautiful setting with two reasonable hotels. Unfortunately lots of tour buses also thought it was a great place to visit.

On the first night as we sat in the lounge, we were invaded by around twenty or so bus trippers who were on a tour of the mountains and lochs of Scotland. It was bad enough that they were a highly vocal group of English tourists, but then they proceeded to turn the TV on for Coronation Street. The next morning we checked out of that hotel and into the other hotel, which was quieter but did not overlook the loch. After a couple of days we decided that we should go home to our lovely new home in the south side of Glasgow.

Before our marriage we had looked at a number of flats around Glasgow, but either could not afford them, or they had sold very quickly. Instead, we found a new complex in the South Side of Glasgow which consisted of around 50 to 60 flats and duplex units. They were co-ownership, which meant that the housing association owned a share of the property. This made it a bit cheaper to buy, which helped us at the time. Fortunately we managed to secure a duplex, which was a lovely modern two-bedroom property. Sandra absolutely loved making this flat into a home. She revelled in choosing curtains, furniture, carpet and all the other housey type things that are needed to make a place liveable. She had very good taste and she made the place lovely, very stylish and elegant. My contribution was cooking. Sandra could not cook, not even simple dishes. She had never needed to cook as her mother had always taken care of that, so she had never learned. Whereas, I had lived in flats, sometimes with friends sometimes alone, so I had needed to learn. Besides my mother was a good cook and I had often hung about the kitchen when she was cooking or baking and picked up a few tips.

At first we were very happy there. We were newly married and living in a beautiful new home. However, I was still friendly with all my old group, all of whom were still unmarried and wanted to continue the life of drink, drugs and rock 'n' roll. So when I invited them all round to our new home, it was a disaster. Well actually it was a wild night and I loved it. Unfortunately, Sandra didn't. The next morning we counted the damage which, although not particularly extensive, was difficult to take for Sandra as this was her 'new' house and she was very proud of it. This event marked a big change in our relationship. Sandra was very houseproud, in my opinion obsessively so. I felt it as stifling, suffocating even, in that I could not leave so much as a newspaper lying around, as Sandra would tidy it away. Even if I wanted to finish reading it later. Her obsessive tidiness versus my casual mess was a flashpoint, and led to many arguments.

The other big issue was my friends. Sandra banned them from the house and asked me not to meet up with them again. This was another flashpoint in our relationship and one that I found difficult. Even though this was only the first year of our marriage, it was marked by many arguments. Often we would argue, and I would storm out and go to the pub round the corner. Sometimes I would meet up with a couple of old friends, but mostly I would drink alone, and increasingly this became a pattern for me. During this time my drinking escalated, as we fell into the pattern of having arguments and me storming out. Indeed, sometimes I would provoke an argument, just so that I could go to the pub.

In hindsight, I can't really blame Sandra for not wanting my friends to come round the house. They were a bit of a wild bunch, who were mostly used to living in rented flats and not having to care for their surroundings. So they had little respect for other people's property and, at that time, neither did I. Although I was now married, I wanted to continue to live and party as if I was still single. I had no real intention of growing up at that time. Sandra on the other hand wanted to have a grown-up relationship, with a proper home and maybe even start a family. The result of these differing attitudes was that the first year of marriage more often resembled a battle ground than a honeymoon.

After only 18 months in our lovely new home, we needed to face the truth, we could not afford to continue living there. The mortgage was very expensive, and I was spending a lot of money on drinking, which just made the financial situation so much worse. So, reluctantly, we sold up and moved in with Sandra's mother Peggy, until we could find another flat. This was a difficult time for all of us. I was still drinking, mostly alone and much preferred to go to the pub and play darts, rather than sit in and watch TV with Sandra and Peggy.

Peggy was a difficult woman to live with. It was her house and therefore she did what she wanted to do, when she wanted to do it, regardless of what anyone else wanted or was doing. A prime example was the night that we had a couple of friends over for a drink. Peggy had been out at the Bingo as usual. However, when she returned, she came into the lounge where we were, carrying a basin of soapy water and began to scrub the couch that our friends were sitting on. They, and we, were so embarrassed that they got up and left. Sandra bundled me into the bedroom to stop me saying anything to her mother and then went back and had a blazing row with her herself.

After almost a year we managed to buy a flat in the Anniesland part of Glasgow. The area was a bit industrialised, with Barr & Stroud (an engineering firm) across the road, but it was also very convenient to both get into and out of Glasgow. The city centre was about three miles away and the west end, Byers Road and the Byre pub about a mile. In the other direction was the main road to Loch Lomond (about 30 minutes) and the Highlands of Scotland. It was also convenient, as Sandra worked in Barr & Stroud, so a very easy commute.

Our ground floor flat was small, just two rooms, one which we used as a large lounge and the second which was the kitchen diner and a large alcove for the bed. It also had a hallway with a bathroom. When we bought it, it required a lot of work to make it habitable. We worked at it tirelessly, because we needed to move out of Peggy's and have a place of our own and some privacy.

Initially, it felt like a new start. We worked together to create a home and a relationship and at first, it seemed to be working out. However, this new start got old very quickly. The general nursing course that I was doing came to an end and I decided that I wanted to do something different. I no longer wanted to work in a hospital, or to work with sick people.

The first job I took was as a double-glazing salesman. It was the late 70s and many people were making a lot of money selling windows. Glasgow had a lot of tenements mostly with single glazed sash windows, so the pickings should be rich for any salesperson. The flaw in the plan was that I am most definitely not a salesman. I had once taken an aptitude test and afterwards the feedback was: "Don't ever go into sales, you will be hopeless at it". It was slightly more tactfully put but that was the gist. Naturally, I did not pay any attention to this assessment.

To ease you into sales, you were first sent out to canvas a neighbourhood and make appointments for the salespeople. I found that I was actually very good at that. I could make lots of appointments very easily. Problem was that whoever made the appointment earned 5% of any subsequent sale, but the salesperson would make 10-15%. Therefore , quite naturally I wanted to be the salesperson. So despite the results of the assessments and the advice of my boss, I got my sales kit and headed off to make my fortune.

I carried on making appointments. I was still very good at it. I was also very good at telling people all about these wonderful 'tilt and open' windows. But I was not good at closing a sale. In fact I was hopeless at it. As soon as I had to ask for money, I became embarrassed and froze, and I think that awkwardness transmitted to the client. However, hope was at hand. I found that after I had had a couple of drinks, closing a sale was much easier and I actually started to make a bit of money. Unfortunately, the logic of the alcoholic kicked in as I reasoned: if I can make a little money when I have a couple of drinks, then if I have a few more, I should be able to make a lot of money. I'm sure you can see the flaw in this reasoning. I can see it very plainly now, but at the time... So ended my career as a salesman.

My next job was in a factory that reconditioned industrial machines such as lathes, as well as making steel plates to clad ships. My job was a jack of all trades.

Essentially, I was a labourer and carried out all the physical, and usually dirty, tasks that were needed. But I was also the van driver and, when needed, the chauffeur for the boss and I also drove the overhead cranes and the mobile crane as well. As jobs go, there was plenty of variety if not a huge amount of money. Sandra preferred me working at this job as, unlike the salesman job it had regular hours and I usually came home afterwards, not to forget, I actually got paid, something which she seemed to feel was important. Unfortunately, the business ran into financial difficulties and, as the last person to join the firm, I was made redundant.

At that time the local psychiatric hospital was advertising for night staff, but I did not want to go back to nursing. Sandra was the only one working and, although I did get some unemployment benefit, she was the breadwinner. I was bored during the day and started drinking quite heavily again, so my benefits went to the pub, therefore I was not contributing to the household. Eventually in frustration and desperation, Sandra filled out an application form for the hospital who, somewhat surprisingly considering my thinly veiled reluctance during the interview, offered me a job.

Yet again we had a new start. It was definitely going to be different this time. And, for a few months it was. The wages in the hospital were good, and I worked extra shifts, which increased our disposable income quite considerably. Then, slowly but surely, my drinking escalated. At first I was still managing to go to work as I was only drinking on my days off but after a while, I was drinking anytime, and taking time off. Now I was using the hospital drugs. I had the keys to the drug cupboard and would view it as a 'pick and mix'. There were lots of tranquillisers and anti-psychotics that were given to schizophrenics and I would help myself to them to steady my nerves. As long as I stayed clear of the controlled drugs, such as morphine, no one would notice. So, if I could not drink, then I doped myself, I was almost always under the influence of something.

We moved to a bigger three-bedroom flat. Yet again, this was going to be different. I suggested that we should start a family, but Sandra somewhat acerbically said that having one child in the family was sufficient for the moment. A bit harsh I thought, even if it was true. Inevitably my drinking escalated again, and Sandra did everything she could to help me. She brought people to the house that might help me, got my mother involved and even called Alcoholics Anonymous for me. I was not interested in changing. As I saw it, the real problem was her. She was boring, bossy and no fun. If it were not for her, I would drink like a gentleman.

Then one day she confronted me in the living room, after I had staggered out of bed with a hangover. Coat on, she had a couple of bags with her: "I don't love you anymore, I don't like you anymore, and I'm leaving before I hate you." And with that, she walked out the door.

Part of me was shocked: how dare she, she'll be sorry leaving a wonderful husband like me. But another part of me cheered inside. Here was what I had told myself I needed; left in peace to live any way I wanted. So now I could drink like a gentleman. So, naturally I headed for the pub to enjoy my newfound freedom. Two hours later I was getting rapidly drunk, as usual. My gentlemanly drinking had lasted approximately 15 minutes. That was the start of a binge that lasted for six weeks, when I was drunk 24 hours a day.

I managed to get myself cleaned up, started going to AA meetings and stayed sober for almost two months.

Then I had a drink and the whole merry-go-round started up again. This time I was drunk 24/7 for two months. That was my last drink!

When I was hospitalised Sandra came to visit and was very supportive. She brought me the things I needed in the hospital, the usual grapes and Lucozade (why do we only drink Lucozade when we are in hospital or ill?), some money and cigarettes. After I came out of hospital and started to get my life together, I asked Sandra if she would like to go out for a meal with me. We took a drive down the Clyde coast to Helensburgh to a little hotel with a nice restaurant. I had decided that during the meal I would ask her if we could get back together and try to make our marriage work. However, before I could ask, she said that she had met someone, and she really liked him. I managed to say that I thought this was nice for her and wished her well for the future of the relationship. And, at the time, I really meant it.

When I returned home later that night, I phoned a friend to let them know how the evening had gone. I told him how well I had done, and how proud I was of myself for how I had responded to the news of her new relationship. Then about 3 a.m. I awoke suddenly with the feeling that someone had just torn the heart out of my chest. The pain was physical and felt initially like a heart attack, but I soon realised that I was now reacting to Sandra's news. I had never been very good with rejection, but then who is? Now I was feeling that rejection without my trusty anaesthetic – alcohol – and it hurt, it really hurt!

From the viewpoint of today, I am glad for the way things turned out. Otherwise I would have attempted to rekindle the relationship with Sandra, and I believe this would have been a mistake. I would have been trying because of the guilt I felt, and out of a sense of duty. But these feelings are neither a recipe for a great romantic love story, nor are they the fuel for reconciliation. More likely a blueprint for resentment.

As I progressed in recovery, I started to realise that Sandra had represented 'safety' for me. She was the one who would be faithful and loyal, and I had needed that assurance at that time, as I had been hurt more than once. What she did not give me was the feeling that my heart missed a beat, that I had trouble breathing when I saw her. She was lovely, both physically and in her personality and she needed someone who would cherish her for that. Unfortunately for her, I needed someone different, someone who would excite me and accept the restlessness that lived inside me and threatened to burst out.

Even now, many years later, I am deeply ashamed of how I treated Sandra. She was a gentle girl who, I believe, loved me deeply and I hurt her. I was not physically abusive or violent, although when I was drinking I had rages and would shout and swear and threaten, and that must have been scary to be around. There was no way she could rely on me for anything. I would have periods of not drinking, but she would never know when, or why, I would start again, but then again neither did I. And when I did drink, I would use the excuse of popping out for milk, a paper, anything and come back days later, sometimes with some very odd people that I had picked up in the pub.

Money was just beer tokens for me, I used to count it as the number of drinks I could get, rather than how many pounds I had. I used the cheque book as a licence to print money and bounced cheques all over Glasgow. When we eventually sold the flat, much of my share went to pay off the debts that I had incurred due to my drinking.

Despite the way I had treated her, we stayed friends for a few years. Eventually she moved away and remarried and, unfortunately, we lost touch. But before she left, I gave her a lift down to Byers Road where we had first met, I was four years sober at the time. As she got out the car, she said cheerio, then she turned back and said, "I'm proud of you". I was deeply touched; it was a special moment for me. Sadly that was the last time we saw each other. I still think of her fondly and dearly hope that she found the person that would make her happy, she deserved that. Maybe one day we will meet again, and I can thank her for all her kindnesses towards me, and apologise properly for my lack of it towards her.

11: Alcohol

Running through my life is a constant travelling companion which has appeared in a variety of guises over the decades. There are times when I have enjoyed it, and all it had to give me. Then there were the times when it almost destroyed me. Then I studied it, and taught others about it, and finally my life has been dedicated to helping others escape its excesses. That companion has been alcohol, and, although it has been broached already, especially in the Sandra chapter, it deserves a chapter all of its own.

In my mid-thirties I was, very reluctantly, at an Alcoholics Anonymous ['AA'] meeting. I was hating being there and felt that it was a complete waste of time. I did not need to be here among these 'wasters'; I was better than that. I did not have a problem, maybe I drank a wee bit too much on occasions, but I was not like these guys, after all they were alcoholics. They said it themselves. Then someone said something that commanded my attention, and his words cut straight through all my cynicism and doubt, and suddenly there came a clarity that I had never had before. He was saying that when he found alcohol, he found the bit that God had left out. Yes, absolutely yes, that's me! It was like someone had just switched a light on, and I finally understood...

When I encountered alcohol in my teens, I was absolutely ripe for it. A heady cocktail of circumstances had all conspired to cripple my self-esteem and make me susceptible to alcohol, and the escape that it offered.

Some, but not all, of these feelings of inadequacy are directly attributable to leaving the seminary and my feelings of failure. Also, I believe that the sheltered atmosphere of the seminary meant that I was less prepared for the more robust atmosphere of life as a developing adolescent than I would have been otherwise. However, I also believe that growing up as an only child contributed greatly, as I did not have the benefit of the experience of sharing a house with siblings that helps to teach us how to interact with others, or compete for attention in a busy, noisy world.

Moreover, another big influence was the grief that affected my mother at the loss of the last child, which resulted in me being sent to live with my aunt for six months. Subconsciously I picked up the idea that I was 'not enough'. Neither of my parents ever said this or even alluded to it in any way, but somehow my exclusion from the circle of grief at that time affected my view of myself, and my place in the family. Then there was her constant over-protectiveness, urging me to "not try too hard as you will just get hurt". That did not exactly build my confidence or self-esteem that I was competent to compete and achieve on my own.

Where this inadequacy was at its most obvious, was in social situations, especially when I was around females. It was difficult for me to talk to females and the more attractive they were, the worse it got. Asking a girl out seemed like a huge risk, which, of course, it is. Yes, I know the image of the gauche teenager struggling to ask a girl out is a cliché. But, for some reason it seemed to be worse for me, rejection seemed more shameful, more painful, and more deserved. It exposed me for the loser that I was. So, it felt deserved, that they were right to reject me.

However, there was good news, the solution was not far away – it was called alcohol!

Alcohol transformed my life in ways that I could never even have imagined. The shyness and social anxiety miraculously disappeared when I drank. The feeling of being invisible and having nothing to contribute to a social occasion, of being stupid and boring, all these feelings vanished. In its place, this magic elixir made me feel confident, intelligent, funny and interesting. Indeed, I was the life and soul of the party. And my awkwardness with females reduced, and I began to feel like God's special gift to women.

Of course, all these feelings were purely subjective, an illusion. I was the only one who experienced my transformation. Other people may have observed a transformation in me, but it was not what I believed it to be. No, they saw someone who was intoxicated, loud, obnoxious and arrogant. Rather than becoming the life and soul of any party they saw a nuisance, someone to be avoided. And as for the females, they seemed to always be interested in something or someone at the other side of the room, in fact they seemed to be interested in anything or anyone at the other side of the room. My reliance on alcohol to 'cure' my social alienation was backfiring spectacularly, but I seemed to be the only person who failed to recognise it. If I did recognise that my behaviour left something to be desired, I always believed that it would be different next time. It never was!

I can't say that I remember my first drink. I do remember that whenever I had a cold, my mother would give me a hot toddy. A toddy was the traditional Scottish cure for colds and flu. It consisted of a small amount of whisky with hot water and maybe lemon and sugar. It was purely medicinal and pretty vile. I'm not sure that it actually had any effect, but sometimes it did seem to help my child self to sleep and heal. So, maybe it was effective after all. Effective or not, Scottish parents of that era certainly believed in the curative power of the toddy. They saw it as a veritable panacea and dosed their children liberally with it. I wonder if there is a link between Scotland's drinking reputation and childhood toddy dosing?

The first drink I remember for pleasure, or social reasons, happened when I was about eight or nine and watching the boxing with my dad. He was a big fan of boxing and had done a bit of boxing in his youth and in the army. That night he had a can of beer, and he poured a tiny drop into a glass with lots of lemonade for me. Then we watched it together. It was a good feeling, we seemed close, like we were buddies, men together doing man things. Despite being such an apparently trivial incident happening all those years ago, I still remember it well. Perhaps in that moment it gave me the connection that, at a very deep level, I unconsciously craved, a feeling of being at peace in the presence of another human.

Whether or not that is rigorously true, I do know that from the very beginning of my drinking, alcohol always had a transformative effect for me. When I drank, I felt that I was more interesting, more intelligent, funnier, more entertaining, more likeable and much more attractive (even irresistible) to women. The fact that most people, especially women, disagreed with all of that was immaterial. What was important to me was the reality inside my head, it was what I thought, what I felt.

Although I did not see it that way, when drinking I often became opinionated and arrogant. I just saw it as my intellect being freed from the shackles of self-doubt. One example by way of illustration happened when I was drinking in a pub on Byers Road, again. This particular pub was not one that I usually frequented, as it was the haunt of students and members of the Young Socialist Party. On this day I was sitting drinking with a group of, mostly younger people and one much older man. I was educating them on politics from my vast knowledge born of reading *The Sun* and *Daily Star*. After a few rounds of verbal sparring the older man got up and went to the toilet. One of the group then turned to me and asked, "Do you know who that is?" I confessed that I didn't. So he said, "That's the professor of politics from Glasgow University." My response was, "Well you would think he would know better, wouldn't you!"

So, while I was intoxicated, other people's views or opinions were of little interest to me, as long as I felt good. As soon as I sobered up, that all changed. Other people's opinions were now crucial, and I found criticism and rejection to be almost crippling, especially towards the end of my drinking.

When I started drinking in my teens, it was generally at the weekend and with my friends. At that time I would never have even considered drinking alone. Drinking was a sociable pursuit, it was reserved for social occasions. All my friends drank and, as far as

I was concerned, they drank the same as me. During my hippy days my drinking escalated, and I also added other substances when available.

When alcohol fell into the damaging zone for me is difficult to say. In the early days after quitting, I reckoned that I had only had a problem for the previous couple of years. However. the longer I stayed sober, the further back I could see there being an issue with alcohol. I now believe that I became psychologically and emotionally dependent on alcohol very quickly, as it allowed me to function in social situations. However, in the final four or five years, I was quite clearly physically dependent also. When I was on a binge, I would suffer rather severe withdrawals, shaking, sweating. These were difficult to cope with, but it was the anxiety and the panic attacks that would really drive my drinking. There were days that I felt that, if I did not get a drink, I would tumble into some mental abyss, never to return. It was terrifying.

After Sandra left me and I lived alone, the flat looked like the bin men made deliveries. There were bottles and cans everywhere, as well as little bits of half-eaten food. I did not eat much when I drank, it just sobered me up, and that was the last thing I wanted. Besides I found it very difficult to keep food down, as the alcohol irritated my stomach.

When I was on a binge, my life consisted of waking up sometime in the morning, actually it was more a case of coming to. Usually I would feel awful, I would be full of fear and have withdrawals. So, I would look to see if there was any alcohol left. If there was, I would try to drink it and very often that would just make me sick. The process of forcing some alcohol down to still the terror was a battle as my body rejected it. This would continue until I could successfully get a drink to go down and stay down. During this exercise I would be naked, because I would sweat so much it was pointless getting dressed as my clothes would be soaked.

Once I had settled my stomach a little, and calmed the fears as much as I could, it was time to go to the pub. But first I needed to get money, and that often meant bouncing cheques, anywhere that would cash one. When I had money in my pocket it was time to pick a pub. I know I was in that one last night, maybe I better go to another, just in case I caused a scene. I suffered badly from blackouts, so the previous evening was often a blank. The first couple of drinks in the pub were difficult, as my body was still rebelling, but after a while I started to feel the first signs of the peaceful numbness washing over my body and mind. Sometimes a couple of guys would come into the pub with a guitar and we would sing some pop songs we all knew, a bit of Simon and Garfunkel, some Beatles anything we could all sing along to. The pubs were open all day, so I did not need to go home. Eventually, when closing time was near, I would head for an off-licence and get some booze to see me through the night. Then I would stagger home and drink till I passed out. The next day was much the same, except the fear was worse, the shame and self-loathing were more than the previous day, and my desire to die, was stronger. This would continue until my body would no longer allow it, and then I had the deeply unpleasant task of drying out and pledging "Never again" – until the next time that is!

My last binge was my worst. It started, as usual with me believing that I could handle it this time, that I knew what to look for, that I could control it. This time I would drink like a gentleman. No great surprise, I couldn't and I didn't. Very quickly I fell back into drinking until I was drunk. The effect that I was chasing in alcohol was always to be found in the next drink. If you picture the cartoon donkey chasing the carrot on a stick, that was me. I never actually wanted to get drunk. Somewhat ironically, I thought drunks were all boring. All I wanted was to feel better about me, and to stop the shame and the fear.

The pattern was the same as before, and the days became a blur. Every day was the same as the last, and I could no longer tell what day it was. I felt that I lived in a constant Wednesday. When I passed out, I could not tell if I had woken up in the morning or the middle of the night. I was becoming further and further divorced from reality, in fact I was no longer sure what was real and what wasn't.

One day, after about eight weeks of drinking solidly (at least I think that it was that long, I honestly don't know) the hospital where I worked phoned up and asked if I was going to come back to work. For some crazy reason, I said that I would be back that night, and that is exactly what I did. I was in charge of a psychogeriatric ward that was mostly quiet. I was in a very bad state but my job was to make sure they all had their medication and then got to bed and slept through the night. So, nothing too demanding and I thought that I could manage to do what was required and then go home and sleep it off.

All went fairly well until Kwame, the nursing officer, came round for the routine visit. He took one look at me and then phoned the office for someone else to come down and be a witness to my condition. By this time I was rapidly going into the DTs (*Delirium Tremens* – severe alcohol withdrawals). Kwame arranged for someone to come and take over from me, then both the nursing officers escorted me to the Chief Nursing Officer's office (Jack Brown). I had not wanted to leave the ward as I held the keys to the drug cupboard and had been going to medicate myself when all the patients were asleep, then just somehow get through the night.

It is all very hazy now, but I remember sitting in Jack Brown's office feeling deeply ashamed. However, it was now obvious to everyone there that I was in a very bad way. I was shaking very violently, sweat was running down my face and I was highly anxious – bordering on panic. Most of what happened in that room was not recorded by my brain, that was just fighting to stop from exploding. However, there was one exchange that proved so significant that even in that terrible condition it still made an impact on me: I turned to Mr Brown and said, "I'm sorry, I'm just a hopeless case." His wonderful reply seemed to penetrate my feelings of self-pity and despair. He said, "That may be true, but you are not a lost cause."

What little I do remember after that was that Mr Brown said that if I was not an employee at the hospital he would have asked the duty doctor to admit me to the alcohol and drug ward as an emergency. He then asked if there was anyone who he could contact that would look after me. During my short time in AA, I had met someone who decided to be my sponsor, Big John, so I gave him John's phone number. John agreed to take me in that night and look after me. So the hospital arranged a taxi to take me to his flat.

When I arrived at John's, he took one look at me and put me straight to bed. By this time I was starting to hallucinate, and all my muscles were going into very painful spasm; I later found out that this was tetany (due to an electrolyte imbalance). John phoned a doctor whose only suggestion was to send me to the psychiatric hospital that I worked in. I declined. After a few days I started to recover. I could get up and walk about and eat a little and drink some fluids without being sick. A couple of weeks later John confessed that he had been terrified all those days, as he was convinced that I was going to die. According to him I was the worst case of alcohol withdrawal that he had ever seen. I believe him.

A couple of days later Jack Brown arranged for me to see the head psychiatrist (Dr Kershaw). He repeated what Mr Brown said, that if I was not an employee of the hospital then he would admit me on the spot, as I was still in the DTs. Instead, he contacted his opposite number on the South Side of Glasgow, Dr Paddy Mullen.

So I left him, got into my car and drove through the Clyde Tunnel, still hallucinating, and arrived at the Southern General Hospital. They welcomed me, took my car keys and wallet away and put me straight to bed and sedated me. It would be 36 hours before I would surface again.

On our first meeting, Paddy Mullen examined me and then declared, "You have brain damage and liver damage. If you continue to take alcohol and drugs, you will be dead in six months." Wow, that was a bit of a wakeup call! Up till that time, I believed that I was indestructible. Sure I would get sick, and it might take me a few days or even a week or longer to recover, but I always did recover. Now here is this psychiatrist telling me that to continue this lifestyle would result in me dying, and soon! A whole lot sooner than I had planned, although often in the middle of a binge I had wanted to die. Whenever I tell people about this incident, they immediately assume that this news of an imminent death was what motivated me to stop drinking. I'm not saying that it had no effect, but it was not the prime reason, that was different.

Maybe it was having some time in hospital to reflect. Or maybe it was waking up to what was happening in my life, the loss of Sandra, the debt I had accumulated.

Or maybe it was that sudden moment of clarity, when the mirror no longer tells me what I want to see. Instead it has the most terrible, horrifying effect, it tells the truth!

I was confronted with a picture of me as totally self-centred. I had always thought of myself as a nice guy, a good husband and a great friend, at least I thought these things when I had had a drink. However, when the need for drink came, especially when I was in the middle of a binge, I would have trampled over anyone just to get a drink. I would have lied or stolen to get the money that would let me get a drink and feel better about myself.

I needed alcohol to remove the terrible anxiety that crippled me at these times. The mirror was showing me a picture of myself, a picture that I really did not want to see. I had never had high self-esteem, nor thought of myself as specially interesting or likeable. However, I had at least consoled myself that I was not a bad person, that I would never deliberately harm anyone. However, this picture showed me something hateful and I vowed that I never wanted to be that person again.

Dying was not what I feared, continuing to live the way I had been, this was my biggest fear. I had used alcohol to make me acceptable to others and, instead, it made me contemptible to me. I could not continue this way! That was my motivation to change.

12: Came to Believe...

Something changed in me while I was in hospital. For the first time in my life I really did not want to drink again, but I was afraid that I could no longer control the cravings. When I left hospital a couple of people, AA members, came alongside me to offer support and I started going to meetings again. When I had attended them previously, I had been dismissive of the people, the programme and the whole movement. I had been arrogant, opinionated and patronising, but now, even though I hated having to admit it, I needed them – desperately needed them.

I was in that hospital for two weeks before Dr Mullen decided that I was fit to be discharged. After leaving hospital I had gone home to my flat. The place was a mess and smelled of booze and neglect. I was now living alone, as Sandra had no intention of returning, and I could not blame her. I wouldn't have come back to me either, if that had been possible. We had agreed to sell the flat and split the proceeds, with me agreeing to pay off the debts that I had accrued through my drinking, from my share. So I set about cleaning up the place and making it fit for viewing.

I was going to meetings every day, sometimes two or even three meetings per day. But even so I still did not feel comfortable, or confident that I could resist drinking. I was not sleeping well. I found it very difficult to get to sleep and when I did sleep, I was having terrible, vivid nightmares. Meeting anyone new was torture, I felt that they could see me for the fraud that I was. Meeting anyone I had known for a long time was almost as bad, I was very uncomfortable in my own skin. Worse, I was scared. I was scared to go out, I was scared to stay in, I was scared to meet people and I was scared to be alone. I was scared that I was going mad and I was scared that the only thing that would save me was to drink, and I desperately did not want to do that.

Three months had passed and I still had not taken a drink, the longest I had remained sober – ever. However, rather than feel increasingly confident, I was feeling more scared. I didn't want to talk about it to other members, as they just told me unhelpful things like, "It's just a day at a time" or "You need to look at the programme." These were things that I did not want to hear; I wanted to hear – it's OK to have the occasional drink, one (or three) drinks now and again won't hurt. Nobody said anything remotely like that, clearly, they had no imagination.

Once I was at a particularly harrowing meeting, where someone told their tragic story of what drink had done to them and, perversely, I felt more and more like a drink as he spoke. I went home to my lonely house and waited for the pubs to shut and remove any choice of going for a drink. Sitting there alone it felt like the walls were closing in on me. I was shaking again and every little noise seemed hugely amplified and threatening. If anyone had asked what I was afraid of, I could not have told them; all I knew was I was afraid, very afraid.

The people in AA, who seemed to be at peace with themselves and the world generally, talked about the programme and how freeing it was. They especially talked about the role of the Higher Power that was described in the second and third steps.

> Step 2: Came to believe that a Power greater than ourselves could restore us to sanity.
>
> Step 3: Made a decision to turn our will and our lives over to the care of God as we understood him.

I struggled badly with these two. Many years before I had turned away from God and I did not care to go back now. I could remember the God of my childhood, I could see the White Fathers preaching Hell and damnation and the wrath of God. And turning to him, even in this desperate time, did not seem like something that I would want to do. However, that night the fear of drinking actually overtook the fear of a vengeful God.

I checked that all doors and curtains were closed and that no one was hiding in the wardrobe. Then, for the first time in many years, I got down on my knees. It was not a long prayer; in fact it was very short. But it was fervent, maybe the most fervent prayer of my life to date. All I said was, "God help me..." then I waited.

I had done my bit, now it was his turn. All I wanted was a little sign that he had heard. Was a choir of angels too much to ask? Or maybe a booming voice saying "This is my beloved son." A fiery chariot even, was that too much to ask? Well nothing happened, absolutely nothing. Finally, I just got into bed and slept.

Next day I was having a good old moan to one of the older members about how the programme was not working. He looked at me for a moment and said, "You're still sober aren't you?" I agreed but pointed out the distinct and extremely disappointing lack of signs and wonders.

"Did you sleep last night?" I grunted that I had slept very well, best in a long time.

"Do you feel like a drink now?" he asked. I didn't and told him so.

"Well what does that tell you? Don't you think that your prayer has been answered?" This was not what I wanted to hear.

No, I wanted the fatted calf killed and celebrations and fireworks in Heaven. I once heard someone say that an alcoholic is an egomaniac with an inferiority complex – they were obviously talking about me. I'm not going to say that I have never felt like a drink since that day, I have. However, I will say that I have never felt an urge or craving for a drink that I felt would overwhelm me. So, that fear of helplessness, that staying sober was not really within my control, had been lifted. Eventually, I did feel that my Higher Power had turned up and saved my life, albeit in a much lower key fashion than I would have liked. My prayer had been answered, maybe not in the way that I wanted, but almost certainly in the way I needed. This is just yet another event in my life that I have only come to appreciate in hindsight.

From that day on, the Higher Power became a major part of my life. He was there during all the major events of my life, weddings, divorces and deaths. He was there to share my joy and he was there when things were difficult, or even just plain boring. However, although he was a constant and a significant part of my life, he remained my Higher Power, faceless and enigmatic. I was still very wary that he was a vengeful God just waiting his time to smite me. So I kept my interactions with him *very* low key and did not have a personal relationship with him, not until much later.

13: Fiona

It was the autumn of 1984 and I had been sober for a few months, my longest dry period in years. My confidence, which was usually alcohol dependent, was non-existent. My flat had been sold, and I was now living with my mother in a one-bedroom pensioner's house in Kirkintilloch. It's fair to say that I was not exactly the most attractive proposition for anyone looking for a relationship.

My friend Michael had taken me under his wing, in these early days of sobriety, and I really appreciated it. We had gotten drunk together in the past and then he had got sober through AA, a year or so before me. At this time, he lived between the nurses' home and his mother's house in Cumbernauld. So we would often meet up at the nurses' home before going off to an AA meeting, or anywhere else, depending what we had decided to do. Sometimes we would just hang around there and socialise with whoever was around at the time. This was where I first met Fiona.

I had seen her in passing before, but the first time we actually interacted was one night Jimmy and I arrived to pick up Michael, only to find out that he was working overtime that night. The nurses' home was very quiet as everyone was either working or had gone out for the night. The only person around was Fiona. Since she was going to be alone that evening, Michael suggested that we take her with us, and she seemed happy at the prospect. So off we went to a little country pub in Kippen, drank coke and played pool and chatted all evening. That was when we found out that she was not a nurse, but instead she was actually a student radiographer, studying for her finals. It was a nice evening and Fiona was good company. We laughed a lot but, in my mind, that was the end of it.

We met again a couple of times when I came to pick up Michael, but I never thought that there was anything between us then, or even that there could be in the future. Indeed, at that time a relationship was well down my list of priorities, as I said, I did not have much to offer. However, one of the nurses was getting married and everyone, including me, was invited to the wedding reception in the evening. I was quite (actually very) anxious about going as I had not socialised much since I had quit drinking, and certainly not at an occasion like a wedding, where drink would be flowing.

Then, just in case my anxiety was not high enough, before we left for the event, Michael and his girlfriend Debbie told me that Fiona had told Debbie that she was attracted to me. This came as a big surprise to me, as we had never spent any time alone together, or made any overtures about getting together. We did become a couple that night, although I'm not entirely sure how it happened!

Months afterwards, when I told her of the conversation that I had had with Michael and Debbie, she looked puzzled and said that she hadn't told Debbie she was attracted to me at all. So, I'm not sure if Michael was just trying to manipulate the situation to motivate me to start dating again. Alternately, it could be that he was trying to set up a social situation for himself, having another couple to socialise with. Whoever was telling the truth or what the motives were, it worked. We started a serious relationship that lasted for around fifteen years. It was not all plain sailing though, as there were a couple of obstacles to overcome before we could settle into the relationship.

The first obstacle was the age difference: Fiona was fourteen and a half years younger than me. So for half the year I was fifteen years older and the other half I was fourteen years older. In the beginning neither of us realised that the gap was quite as large. She had thought that I was younger, and I had thought she was older. Although when we did realise the age difference it was an initial shock, we actually found that it was not a problem. We had so many things in common, taste in books and music, that the age did not seem to matter.

The second obstacle was a bit more of a problem: there was a boyfriend, Tom, in the background. He was also a radiographer. The reason he was not around was because he had gone to Ireland to find jobs and accommodation for both of them. A few weeks into our relationship, she announced that the boyfriend had found them jobs and a flat in Ireland and now wanted her to join him there.

When we talked over what to do, I said that she needed to go over there, see him and figure out what she wanted. Did she want to spend her life with him? Was this how she wanted her future to be? If it was, then she needed to go and make it happen.

So off she went, and I missed her. I had grown fond of having a girlfriend, of the companionship and the intimacy. She had really helped to put some life back into me at a fairly bleak season of my life. After a week or so I had hoped to hear from her but I heard nothing. Then the following week Michael and Debbie said they wanted to speak to me, Debbie had received a letter from Fiona. It seemed that when Fiona had arrived in Dublin, Tom had proposed, and they had become engaged. She was coming back to Glasgow the following week to collect all her stuff and then go back to Dublin and get married. She had asked Debbie to let me know. I'm not sure what I expected to happen, but whatever it was that was probably not it!

I was disappointed at the outcome, but not entirely surprised, after all there was the age gap and the fact that Tom and she had been a couple for a lot longer than we had. So I was not exactly broken hearted. That night Michael and Debbie worked on me, encouraging me to fight for the relationship. All the time they kept playing the same song over and over – Phil Collins, *Against All Odds*. Can't say I was ever a big fan, but his lyrics and music just penetrated, and I finally promised to go and meet Fiona at the station; just as long as they turned off the music!

So I picked her up at Central station in Glasgow and we drove somewhere we could talk without any interruption. How long we talked and what was said are details that are lost in the intervening years. The upshot was that we renewed our relationship, and she wrote to Tom to break off the engagement. About a week later we returned from a night out to find Tom waiting for us, well, to be accurate, waiting for Fiona. They went off into a room and talked for what seemed like ages. Later Fiona emerged and asked if I would give Tom a lift across Glasgow, to where his mother would pick him up. That has to be one of the most uncomfortable car journeys I have ever been on, and I've been in an Egyptian taxi through Luxor. The oppressive silence in the car was only broken by terse directions from Tom in the back seat. When we arrived at the meeting point Tom's mother was there in the full "you've hurt my precious son mode". I bundled Fiona back in the car, away from the abuse that this lady was screaming at her. Looking back, and even at the time, I couldn't entirely blame the lady, her son had been hurt. I can just imagine that under those circumstances my mother would have been the same, but hopefully with a bit more dignity and a lot lower volume.

We were both a bit shaken up, particularly Fiona. The last thing we wanted was to go back to the nurse's home and answer all the questions that our friends, particularly Michael and Debbie, would have for us. Instead, we decided to drive across the city and down to Luss on Loch Lomond. It had been a memorable night and it needed something magical to end it, marking the start of a new era. We parked down by the water's edge, put some Pink Floyd on the stereo, cuddled into each other and watched the sun rise over the loch, and it did not disappoint.

While our relationship flourished and grew stronger, I was still living with my mother, when I wasn't living in the nurse's home that is. That was about to change. One of the last things that Sandra and I had done as a couple was to put a deposit down to reserve a house on a small new estate that was being built in the Anniesland area of Glasgow. Planning and other issues had meant that the building was delayed for a couple of years. With the split in our marriage, Sandra had gone to our solicitor and cancelled her share of the house. When the solicitor contacted me to ask if I also wanted to cancel, he advised me that in those intervening years although house prices had increased massively, our deposit had locked the price at the original levels. So it would represent a huge bargain. For that reason, and because I needed a place to live, I took over the house.

Finally, the house was ready, and I moved in. It is easy to pinpoint the day; it was 13th July 1985. Live Aid was happening as we moved the furniture in. The first thing I did was to prop the TV up on a box, so that we could watch the concert while we emptied the other boxes and moved furniture. Fiona rolled up her sleeves and unpacked boxes and helped put the place together, ably helped by Michael and Debbie and a couple of others.

That night Fiona stayed the night, and the next night, and the next and the one after that. After a couple of weeks I asked her, "why don't you just move in?" So she did, and she never moved out again, that is until we moved house thirteen years later.

Life was good. We had a three-bedroom house in a nice location, the canal was about a hundred yards away, with nice walks along the towpath and there was a wild park on the other side of it. If we walked in the other direction there were shops, pubs and restaurants and transport into the city. If we drove the other direction, we could be on Loch Lomond in just over half an hour. It was a good place to live, even if it was still a bit of a building site.

Fiona passed her finals and got a job working as a radiographer in Monklands Hospital and I continued working as a psychiatric nurse, on night shift at Gartnavel Royal Hospital, the local psychiatric hospital just over a mile away. We were happy, and in love and we could now carve out the life that we wanted.

I attended Alcoholics Anonymous at least once a week, usually more often. Michael and I, with another school friend of Michael's, Jimmy, opened a new group. Although this was much more of a discussion group, in the style of the original meetings, many old timers criticised it as not being in 'proper' AA format. Nevertheless, it became very popular and helped many people get sober, especially those who struggled with the more traditional chairing and sharing meetings.

When I got sober there were many things I wanted to do, things that I had sat around in pubs and talked about doing. So, now that I was sober and had put in a bit of time, I thought that this would be a good moment to start doing some of these things. The first of these was to get out into the countryside, the mountains and lochs, and explore more than I had ever done. Credit to Fiona, she was game to get out there with me; it would have been much harder for me if she had not been interested. At the beginning we walked some of the many woodland trails that Scotland has in abundance. This was very sweet for me because many of the initial trails were in the area of outstanding beauty called the Trossachs. This was an area that my dad had introduced me to when we went out for rides on his scooter. Now I could actually get into these trails and explore more than I had ever done with him.

After a while we became more adventurous and tackled a few higher hills, not actual mountains, more like the nursery slopes. Slowly but surely we were getting fitter and increasing in stamina and confidence, but it was still a bit incongruous to see us sitting on top of a hill, or maybe just halfway up, with Fiona puffing on her asthma inhaler while I puffed on my cigarette. Then we bought better equipment and started climbing the mountains. Muriel Gray put it beautifully in her book when she talked about the different kinds of climbers, she called them Ramblers, Scramblers and Danglers. We were definitely, ramblers and occasionally scramblers, but never danglers.

Most of our weekends, if we were not working, we could be found in the mountains. At first we were fair-weather walkers, but I decided that we needed to increase our skill level and signed up for a winter skills course in Glencoe. It was great weekend for it. We arrived in a blizzard, in fact they actually closed the road through Rannoch Moor just as we passed through. What was good about that was that we would not be short of snow to practice the winter skills. As it turned out, there was a bit too much of it and too fresh, so we just sank into the deep snow, rather than sliding down the slopes. Nevertheless, it was great weekend as we learned about navigation and how to survive in the mountains if we were trapped by the weather. Some useful skills, no doubt, but some which you prayed that you would never be called to use, but it would be better to know, just in case.

I loved the mountains in the winter. There were fewer people around, so we had the place to ourselves. My favourite time was when there had been a new snowfall. The mountains looked majestic, beautiful and pristine. Ours were the only footsteps and it felt like we were the only people in the world, this was a great feeling. Like walking in the garden of Eden, but you definitely needed a few more clothes than a fig leaf!

Did Fiona enjoy our times in the mountains as much as I? Certainly at the time, I believed that was the case. However, whether she did or not, and I have no real way of knowing now. She was my companion and fellow explorer, she supported me in what I wanted to do, and for that I will always be grateful.

She was also very supportive of me returning to education and, although I know that my studies sometimes ate into our together time, she seemed to understand the need I had to prove something to myself. When I won the Scottish Office fellowship, she was supportive of me resigning my permanent job to study for a PhD, even though there was no guarantee that I would have a job at the end of it. Again, I was, and still am, grateful for this support.

Support was not just in one direction. Over the years I supported her in many ways. A simple example would be that when we first became a couple, although she could swim a bit, she was afraid to swim out of her depth. On a catamaran trip round Zakynthos in Greece, we dropped anchor at the iconic bay you see on the adverts for Greek holidays. The one surrounded by sheer cliffs with a wreck of a ship on the beach. Many people, including myself swam ashore but Fiona would not. So, when I returned to the boat, I persuaded her to get into the water and swim around the boat and then through between the keels. After a few times where I literally, supported her, she began to overcome her fear.

Later, I persuaded her to take scuba diving lessons. We both trained and became qualified divers, in Loch Fyne in Scotland, which, while it is beautiful, is cold and can be very murky from the peat and heather that is washed into the loch from the snow melt in spring. A week later we were jumping off a boat in the Maldives to dive in the Indian ocean. The contrast was enormous. From not being able to swim out of her depth, Fiona subsequently went on to dive all over the world.

Education was another area of her life where I supported, encouraged and, at times, even bullied her. Her radiography qualification was a Diploma and I encouraged her to upgrade to a degree through the Open

University. Later, obtaining this degree enabled her to get a job as a university lecturer in the radiography department.

There is a deep irony about my supporting her to become a diver and to study at the Open University. For it was at an Open University summer school that she met the man who is her current husband, and their point of connection was that they both were scuba divers!

So what happened? How did this, outwardly at least, idyllic relationship come to an abrupt and painful end? At the time, I did the time-honoured thing, I blamed her. Of course I did, she was the one who went off with a toy boy (turned out he was 22 years younger than me). So naturally, it must have been her fault. But later, once the anger faded and life in all its rich experiences continued, the answer to what happened did not look quite as clear cut. Let me try and analyse/explain what I think happened, bearing in mind that this view is subjective. If we asked Fiona, she might, OK probably would, give a slightly different version.

For much of my life prior to meeting Fiona and since, I have been a bit of a loner. I tended to travel by myself, often went on holiday by myself. Not because I had no one who wanted to go with me, I had a few offers, for me it was just easier. I did not have to wonder if the others were wanting to do something else or go somewhere else; I did not need to feel guilty that I was being selfish by doing what I wanted. I remember seeing a quote by Groucho Marx which said "I would not join any club that would have me as a member". This absolutely resonated with the feelings of unworthiness that plagued me from, maybe before I went to the seminary, certainly after I left it.

When I discovered alcohol and drugs I found the solution to that problem, it was liquid personality, tablets of likeability, the elixir of charm. It allowed me to talk to people, especially females. I could be sociable and even comfortable in company. When I had to give up drink and drugs, I lost that ability to alter how I felt about myself instantly (or at least fairly quickly). I had to fall back on my natural reserves, which I always felt were pretty meagre.

When Fiona and I started together, I found it difficult to believe that she could be interested in me. The 'Greek Chorus' in my head continually shouted abuse about my weight (I *was* overweight then), my age (in comparison to hers) and downright lack of personality (which was not entirely fair, but I did struggle to express it). At the time when we moved in together, I was working on night shift at the hospital. Some nights the Greek Chorus ['GC'] were dramatically active filling my head with pictures of Fiona rolling around in our bed with some guy that had just been waiting round the corner for me to leave for work. At the beginning of our relationship, some nights when I was leaving for work, she would cry and tell me how much she missed me, these nights the GC was generally quiet. Other nights as I left for work, we would hug and I would say "I love you:" when she answered "I love you too" the GC was usually well behaved. But the nights when she did not reply or said something, anything else instead, the GC would be in full voice to the extent that in the morning I would find myself looking for signs that someone else had been there.

Now, I'm fully aware that this insecurity was nothing to do with Fiona. This was my own demons, and I needed to deal with them. My doubts were rooted in my own sense of worth, not in her fidelity, so I needed to start working on my self-esteem and self-worth, and this I did. Otherwise my jealousy could have torn the relationship apart. In hindsight perhaps I did too good a job, and years later I became too complacent and missed all the signs. Certainly one of my friends asked me many times during the breakup 'how did I not see the signs'. My answer was that I was not looking, I trusted her. Oh the irony!

Looking back to our engagement: my first proposal was maybe not the most romantic. We had been together a couple of years; we were in bed and had just made love and were still in the throes of passion, so I asked her to marry me. She said no! That wasn't so good. However, she said that she was happy as things were and just was not ready. Over the next couple of years I asked her again, twice. And twice I got the same answer. Oh well.

On February 29th 1988 (leap year) I came home from work and she had laid out my suit and said that I needed to get dressed quickly, as there was a taxi coming. The taxi took us to The Buttery, a very upmarket restaurant in Glasgow that I had taken her to after she had come back from Dublin. During the meal she proposed and, of course, I said yes. Later that year we were in Olympia, Greece where we bought an engagement ring. We were in a very good place in our relationship, life was good and the GC was quiet, at any rate most of the time.

What I didn't realise at that time was that I was not the only one with a very active GC. We were to find that Fiona had a world-class one with a virtuoso soloist. However, like so many people, I did not recognise this at the time and certainly did not appreciate the destructive force that it would have on us both.

After their initial awkwardness of the breakup from Tom and the revelation of the age difference, her parents seemed to become very fond of me and were delighted with the news that we were engaged to be married soon. Fiona's mother phoned us and invited us to visit for the weekend "To talk about the wedding." Some years previously, Fiona's granny had said that she would pay for her wedding, whenever that day came. So, naturally we were expecting them to discuss the plans and tell us how they were going to contribute to the big day. The weekend dragged on and no one mentioned anything about the wedding, absolutely nothing. Fiona was understandably upset, and I was puzzled, we were there at their invitation. So, I decided that I would confront them about it. But Fiona stopped me saying, perhaps wisely, that they probably would not forgive what they might see as a demand for money. So nothing was ever said about how the wedding would be paid for or even any of the plans regarding the details.

I felt so sorry for her. This is a day that most young women want to share with their mother. They want to plan and shop with their mother but she did not get any kind of reaction at all. After this snub I began to notice other things that contributed to the songs that her GC would sing. It is a common mistake to think that GCs only have one song, they usually have a rather extensive repertoire, that can change over the years. Although they do generally have their 'greatest hits' which they trot out most regularly.

The showstopper for Fiona's GC was that old standard "You're not beautiful or loveable". It is a tragedy that this is a legacy that so many mothers give to their daughters. It is not deliberate, and they would almost certainly be horrified if they were told that this is what they were doing. Sadly the origin is their own mother and grandmother who have passed it down through the generations. A prime example of it came when Fiona got her wedding dress and wanted to show her mum. Her mother looked at it and then came the exquisitely crippling phrase "You look lovely my dear..." [pause, all good, the compliment has gone in: now comes the kicker] "...but see, when I was your age ...." It does not really matter what follows that phrase, the effect is devastating, the message is crystal clear, you will never be as good/beautiful/talented as me. I would love to have met that great-great-great granny – she must have been really something to see, a veritable goddess. Of course this had not been the first, or last, time that Fiona would hear this phrase. That was the problem, she had probably grown up with it, hearing it like a mantra until she believed it deep in her soul, and then her GC picked up the mantra and continued to remind her, in case she should forget and mistakenly feel good about herself.

The other showstopping song from the GC was "You are not important!" Again, this is a crippling and hugely hurtful song. For Fiona the origin could be found in the relationship with her young brother Brian. He had suffered compromised kidneys as a child, which meant that he had slight learning difficulties which would prevent him ever living an independent life. He also needed to have dialysis. But because his parents, well his mother, did not want him to be hospitalised, or to have to make regular visits to have renal dialysis, she arranged to carry out Peritoneal Dialysis (a version of dialysis that can be done at home). Unfortunately, the procedure needed to be done three times a day and was hugely time consuming. The result was that, understandably the routine of the household revolved around Brian and his needs and Fiona and Max (her dad) seemed to be very much an afterthought. Prior to Brian being born (about five years) and subsequently needing so much input, Fiona was the sole child and presumably received a lot of love and attention. But now her place had been usurped, so understandably Fiona felt neglected and unloved and craved attention to prove the GC wrong.

For my own GC repertoire, one of the strongest refrains was "You need to take care, don't overstretch yourself." This made me feel smothered, almost suffocated at times. This, of course, was my mother's mantra and I had resisted it for years, often by running away. For Fiona to cope with her GC, she needed validation, lots of validation that she was loveable and loved. At the beginning of our relationship that was rather flattering, that someone would want my attention so much. It helped to quell the GC in me and make me feel worthy and likeable.

Unfortunately, in later years her need bumped up against my GC which was singing the smothering song, so it made me want to run. For that reason, I started to neglect her emotionally and physically. This must have been very difficult for her, and so she sought comfort elsewhere, finding a guy who was a few years younger than herself to help silence her GC. But that was over a decade away.

The wedding went well. Everyone seemed to enjoy themselves. Everyone that is except me. Like many weddings, we had the ceremony and the wedding breakfast with only a small group of people attending. Then in the evening we had a reception for all our friends and relations, which was quite a crowd. The early part of the wedding was quite relaxed. The evening was loud, lots of music, drinking and dancing. I felt obliged to go round and talk to every table and thank them for their gift and/or for coming. This is a lot of strain for a sober introvert, and it took its toll. I could feel 'trapped' waves washing over me, which is terrifying, and I wanted to run, or just curl up in the foetal position. I managed to get through the wedding without panic and without a drink, but these feelings lasted for three days, and only just wore off when we were in Greece for our honeymoon, and I could come back to normal.

It was one of the most severe attacks I had experienced since getting sober and at the time I could not decide if the feelings were caused by all the socialising, or because I now felt 'trapped' in a marriage. Looking back now, I believe the answer was yes, it was both. It is a paradox that I have noticed about myself, that I long for something, like a relationship, and strongly believe that this is what is going to make me live happily ever after. Then if I actually get what I want, I can feel all my options have been removed, and I'm trapped. It's what psychologists might call *post-decisional regret*. Another girlfriend often commented that I could happily browse through shops for hours without buying, whereas she needed to buy something. I enjoy the feeling of having lots of possibilities and when I make a decision I lose that feeling. To this day I value keeping my options open.

The next few years were good for us. We both continued working in our respective hospitals, at weekends, we went off to the mountains, even bought a caravan in Inverary, to be closer to them and we holidayed mostly in the Greek Islands. Although, one time we went to Israel instead, to Eilat, which was exciting, plus I arranged a trip to Petra for Fiona's birthday.

I applied for, and duly won, one of the Fellowships that the Scottish Office offered each year to NHS workers. This allowed me to quit my job and study full-time at Glasgow University for a doctorate in psychology which was awarded in 1993. On the completion of my PhD, I was awarded a Senior Research Fellowship to carry out research on alcohol treatment. Then I obtained a lecturing post at the Centre for Alcohol and Drug Studies at Paisley University, which meant that I had a regular salary and we could think about moving house. I wanted to move out of Glasgow and into the country. At heart I have always been a country boy and never been very much at home in cities. We moved to a village called Chapelton, which had one pub, a post office and around 200 houses. Fiona seemed keen on the prospect at the time, after all it was nearer her work, but looking back I'm less convinced. She is an extrovert and loves people and parties, I'm an introvert and like small intimate social occasions, like dinner parties. Moving to the country probably suited me much more than it suited her. However, I do not remember her ever voicing any reservations about the move at the time. But like many important things in our life, we did not sit down and have a serious discussion about the move.

When my boss had to take sick leave from work to have a hip replacement, I had to take on more responsibility. I also used the opportunity to push through some projects that I had been trying, without much luck, to get him to OK for some time. I started the process of turning our course into a distance learning format, to make it accessible to many more students. In fact it increased the number of students fivefold. Also I organised an international conference, bringing some of the biggest names in the addiction field to Paisley. Obviously, along with my other duties this took time and I was staying later at work, not arriving home till late evening. Consequently, Fiona felt increasingly neglected physically, emotionally and socially. I, on the other hand, was excited. I was making a real difference to the course and how it was run and creating a real buzz about the upcoming conference.

As I saw it then, her disapproval of my absence felt like she was trying to control me and I began to resent her and even at times wished she was not in my life. I did not want anything to happen to her, I just wanted to be left alone to get on with my projects, and she was in the way. The GC were singing the smothering song and I wanted to run. All too soon I got my wish. It was the 2000 AD. We had made it into a brand-new millennium, the computers had not crashed, and apart from having to keep remembering that the year started with a '2' rather than a '1,' life seemed to go on exactly as before. Only, for us, it didn't.

On the 6th of January, Twelfth Night, I was packing away the Christmas tree for another year. Fiona came home from work and watched me for a minute, then she made her announcement. "I'm leaving."

"Sorry, you're what?"

"I'm leaving. I'm not happy and I need some time to myself. I have rented a place. Please don't try to find me. I'll be in touch."

"Is there someone else?"

"No, I just need time."

The ground seemed to shift beneath my feet. True I had found her neediness difficult to take and I had wanted her to be somehow not there. But not like this! This was not what I wanted at all. It was one thing me not wanting her, it was a whole different ball game her not wanting me! What was it about me that after nearly 15 years together that made her want to up and leave? And, why should I not try to find her, did she see me as some sort of abuser? There was only one thing to do, that was beat myself up, something that I had raised to an art form over the years.

I was left without answers as it was clear that she couldn't or wouldn't talk to me about it, so I asked her if she would talk to one of my AA friends. What I found out from that conversation spelled the end of our relationship. It transpired that there was actually someone else; worse still, he was not the first. I don't know how many 'someone-elses' there had been, but apparently this one was different, this one was serious.

We made a date to go out for a meal and talk. Sadly, that definitely did not go well. I went to pick her up from her rented flat and she was still getting ready, so she told me to have a seat in the living room. There staring at me was a very large framed photo of the new boyfriend, and an even larger valentine card. It felt like my nose was being rubbed in the situation, it felt insensitive in the extreme. The result was that dinner was a less than cordial affair, I was angry and she was acting like some spoiled teenage girl defying her parents with an unsuitable boyfriend, which just made me angrier. I just did not recognise the woman I had lived with for all these years.

If I had wanted to try and save the marriage before that dinner, I had no desire to do so afterwards. It had felt for some time that the age gap was widening, rather than narrowing. I'm not sure if I was behaving older, I probably was, but I do know that she was definitely acting more childish. That night the age gap felt like a gaping chasm. I asked if she was going to go and live with him. She said she didn't know. My parting words to her sealed our fate, or maybe it had been sealed long before, and I was the only one who did not know it. I said, "You better go and find out if he will have you, because I won't."

I don't know if there had been a chance of a reconciliation, whether we could have managed to patch up the marriage, after all we had been through, all we had meant to each other. But what I realised that night was that I could not live with the lack of trust. If she was late home, or if she said that she was going away for the weekend with the girls, what would I feel like?

Would I believe her? I mean, really believe her. My GC would be giving glorious concerts with many encores, and I believe that the suspicion would have certainly killed the relationship. It was better, maybe more painful, but in the long run, better to end it there and then, rather than face the tragic death of a thousand cuts that would have ensued.

Unsurprisingly, I was sad that it ended the way that it did. Like so many relationships and marriages that hit the rocks, we may have managed to salvage ours by communicating about our feelings, fears and hopes much better than we had done, and much earlier in the relationship, rather than wait till it was too late. The real sadness for me was the lies and deceit. When the story actually came out, I felt that I had been kept in the dark, not to protect me as she suggested, but as a safety net in case her new relationship did not work out. Then she could stroll back and say I've had some time out, but now I'm back. That left a bitter taste in my mouth, and it was definitely not a role that was in any way acceptable to me.

That sour taste was increased on the last day we saw each other. As you can imagine, it was so sad going through our things and deciding what items belonged to each of us, the books, the records. Every item had a story and we both cried a lot during the process, as our past was divided up on the table. However, one thing that became obvious was that she was completely shedding that past. When we came to items that had sentimental value, photographs or letters to each other, even our wedding photos, she did not want any of them. It felt that I was being erased. One thing though, she did grab. It was one of the first things she took from the house, and that was the diving gear that I had bought her for Christmas. She would now use it to go diving with her new man. Again, it was hard to recognise this woman sitting across from me. As part justification, referring back to her ex-fiancé Tom, she said, you knew what I was like. Maybe I did, but actually I thought, or at least, I had hoped that she had changed after 15 years. I certainly know I had. As I said, I was sad that it ended that way.

Today I am really sorry for neglecting her and for not recognising nor meeting her deep needs, and also for not talking about the state of our marriage much earlier. I accept full responsibility for my part in our breakup. Sadly, I'm not convinced that she accepts responsibility for her part. But if the parting had been done with a bit more sensitivity, maturity and honesty, maybe we could have remained friends. That would have been nice.

Don't get me wrong, we did not part on bad terms. We conducted our business dealings (selling the house, splitting the assets) amicably and with dignity. In fact our solicitor remarked that he had dealt with married couples that were still together who argued more than we did. In the breakup we just divided everything down the middle, neither of us had any desire to make a difficult situation worse.

Over the intervening years, we have been in contact occasionally and these times have been amicable, and we are on each other's Christmas card list. I wish her well, and dearly hope that she found someone who provides for all her needs, and can silence her GC. She deserves that.

14: Academia

One aspect of my life where I felt some discontent was in the realms of education. At school, through primary up until early secondary, I had always been considered to be clever. However, my academic achievements fell well short of my promise. Indeed, after returning from the seminary I had no interest or motivation for school and left with very few qualifications, and even less ambition. Being around people who were, or had been, at university made me feel ashamed and envious. It felt like, although not usually true, that they were looking down on me and thinking less of me. The reality was that it was me who looked down on me, and I strongly felt the need to prove myself, to other people but mainly to myself. So, one of my ambitions after getting sober was to return to education, study for a degree and test my capabilities.

Fortunately for me, the Open University was well established in the UK and the open entrance requirements allowed me to sign up for a course. For some strange reason that escapes me now, I initially enrolled in a science foundation course, which was odd since having been in the seminary, I had never studied science. Some of the course I enjoyed, for example the Earth Sciences and Physics and some of which I was less keen on, namely Chemistry and Biology. Although I had been leaning towards continuing with a degree in Maths and Physics, I finally decided that I should study Psychology. Since I was a psychiatric nurse, working in a psychiatric hospital, it seemed like a much more logical direction to go in. Besides, I had always had an interest in how people work.

I found that I enjoyed the subject as, for me, it did not require a great deal of studying. I found that it was the kind of subject that I could read through and understand, and if I understood it, then I retained it. So, even though I was working full time, in a relationship, had a busy social life and attended AA meetings, I was still managing to get good grades and was on course to get a 2.1 degree. This grade would allow me to follow my new ambition, to become a Clinical Psychologist. To test the water and see if this was a viable goal, I made an appointment to go and see the head of the Clinical Psychology course at Glasgow University. It was a productive meeting and, although they could not actually guarantee me a place, they said that, with the combination of my grades and experience that they would look very favourably on my application. It felt that my life was sorted now. I only had one year of my degree to complete, and then I could start on the clinical course.

Like much of my life, the plans I made and how things actually turned out bore little resemblance to each other. One of my Open University tutors (Barry Jones) was also a lecturer at Glasgow University, and he sent me a message to meet up. It turned out that he had been impressed by my essays and thought that I might be interested in a study he was involved in. At the time he was working with another nurse who had been awarded a fellowship from the Scottish Office. They were working on a project that was very fashionable at that time – Nursing Informatics – basically an inventory of what nurses do, how long it takes to do it, and whether it could be done more efficiently.

Barry asked if I would be interested in becoming part of the study and helping with the data collection. At the time, I was keen to be involved in research, as I really wanted to extend my experience. I was already doing some part-time work for a social research agency, interviewing for the National Crime Survey (one of the largest annual social science data collections in the UK). So being involved in Barry's study seemed like a useful move. Since it was a voluntary, unpaid position, part of the carrot to become involved was that he would support an application to the Scottish Office for a NHS fellowship. That would allow me to continue to be involved in research and also register for a higher degree. So, I was happy to be involved, as this represented my possible entrance into academia.

I can't say that I found the work to be particularly interesting. The study was a bit too mundane for me as there was no real theoretical basis for the work. It was just a matter of watching nurses at work, describing what they did in each five-minute period and crunching the data to find patterns, basically a time and motion study. However, since it would be a route into higher study, I saw it as a means to an end.

When the NHS advert appeared, I applied for the fellowship. The competition was fierce, as only three fellowships were awarded each year. Although I did get through to the interview stage, and although it did seem to go well, unfortunately I did not get the award. The feedback that I was given was, that the project was essentially Barry's, and that my involvement in it would be as an employee on his work. While that situation may have given me some good experience, the scope for personal development as an independent researcher would be limited. Naturally I was disappointed at the time, but in hindsight, they were completely correct, and I am now massively relieved. I would have been bored rigid, and the rejection allowed me the time to subsequently develop my own project.

My main interest at that time was the rehabilitation of psychiatric patients back into the community. This was the late 1980s, the time of the clearance of the psychiatric hospitals and the introduction of "Care in the Community". It seemed at the time, on paper at least, that we were coming out of the Dark Ages regarding psychiatry, and emerging into a newer, more hopeful age where psychiatric illness would be treated differently, more humanely. Unfortunately, as with many initiatives of this type, the reality was rather different to the rhetoric. In the enthusiasm (or maybe more accurately the political pressure) to get this new policy to work, patients who had been institutionalised for years, decades even, were being discharged to take their rightful place in society. Problem was that society was not ready for them, come to think of it, many of the patients were not ready for that society. The infrastructure of support was not in place (decades later it still isn't...) and there were few, if any, safety nets for the patients that struggled with the difficult transition from a highly organised, institutional environment to independent living in a rapidly changing community. So, in my wisdom, I decided that my project should be to produce an assessment tool that would measure how ready a patient was for rehabilitation and, if there was a deficit, what was needed to ensure that they were successful. Ambitious yes, but a worthwhile challenging project (at least I thought so).

I was still working full-time in the hospital at the time, which meant that any development of a project really needed to be in an environment that would allow me to both work and collect data. Unfortunately, the hospital management clearly were not listening to my needs. Instead they decided to shuffle the staff "to freshen our experience". To my horror, I was allocated the Alcohol and Drug Unit. There was not another ward in the hospital that was less appropriate for the study I wanted to do, and nobody wanted to hear about my issues. When I presented my case for special treatment, the management pointed out that they paid my salary and that they could, and would, place me where I was most needed. Which was an accurate, if somewhat blunt and unsympathetic, statement of the situation.

The last thing that I wanted to study was alcoholism and/or drug addiction. Both of these issues had played such a large part in my life. Indeed they had almost ended it. So, understandably, I was keen to leave that part of my life behind and move on to a new chapter.

This is one of those situations where, in hindsight, it felt like God was moving and gently guiding my path. As I said, I could see this guidance in hindsight, but at the time I just wanted to throw a tantrum, as it felt that I was being thwarted in my true ambitions. However, as the saying goes, "If life gives you lemons, then make lemonade". So that is what I did, obviously not literally! But I thought that it was a positive view of the situation, as well as being a fitting quote for an alcoholic. Since I was stuck in the Alcohol and Drug ward, it seemed logical to start looking at creating an AA assessment instrument that would provide some meaningful information about addiction. The big research question at that time (the end of the 80s) was "Why do people drink". The rationale was that, if we find out what they want from alcohol then, we can offer them a non-harmful way of achieving the same goal. For example, if someone used alcohol as a stress reliever, then we could teach other methods of stress relief, such as meditation. Sounds sensible, but the big flaw is, that while it takes months to learn meditation, you can get as stress relieved as a newt in half an hour down the pub. So my question was not "Why do people drink?" but rather "Why do people not stop drinking?".

You will almost certainly be relieved to hear that I am not going to inflict the theory and data of my thesis here. Suffice to say that I put together a tool to measure motivation to change in problem drinkers. I then applied again for a Scottish Office Fellowship and this time I was successful. I contacted the bosses of the hospital where I worked and requested that they second me to study. That way, I would have a job to return to, and they would have someone with skills that could be used somewhere within the organisation. I saw this as a win–win situation, thankfully they didn't. They refused, which meant I would be jobless when I completed my PhD. After some serious thinking and a discussion with my wife (Fiona) we decided that this was far too good an opportunity to miss. The Scottish Office were paying my full salary and picking up the tab for any expenses while I studied. The future could take care of itself when it came. So, I resigned from the hospital and enrolled full time at Glasgow University as a PhD student in the Department of Psychology.

Right from the beginning I loved it. I mean really loved it. It was hard to believe that they ('they' being the Scottish Office) were actually paying me to do this. I regularly said to anyone who would listen (obviously except the Scottish Office) that I would happily pay to just be allowed to do what I was doing. This was one of the happiest times of my life. The academic life really suited me and no one pushed me to do much. No one needed to, I was highly motivated. There were the classes on advanced statistics, most people dreaded them, but strangely I enjoyed them, mainly because I could recognise how they could be used to answer the many questions that I had. In fact, I took to the subject so well that I was asked to provide a workshop for the entire department, students, lecturers and professors, on how to use Multiple Hierarchical Regression and why most researchers get it wrong. Initially this was a bit intimidating, for me to be lecturing to the faculty, but as it went on, I found that I really enjoyed teaching and, as it turned out, I even seemed to be quite good at it. As part of the department, I was given more teaching practice, lecturing to undergraduates on research methods and statistics, as well as the Psychology of Addiction.

My research was proving to be very successful. Indeed, two of the main metrics for academic success are publications and conference papers. On both of these metrics I was excelling and started to build a reputation, both as a conference speaker and an authority on addictive behaviour. The one fly in the ointment was that I discovered that my fellowship was not going to be extended to three years. Previous holders of the Scottish Office Fellowships had applied and were routinely given a third-year extension, so they could finish their PhD. Unfortunately, the Scottish Office cutbacks meant that this extension was no longer being granted. This news caused a bit of a panic as I would not have the statutory three years to finish my PhD, and I had no job to go to at the end of the fellowship.

The first thing I did was to petition the university to submit my thesis early. Although this was not a common request, they did grant it. The second thing was to lock myself away and write the thesis. Fortunately, I had collected most of the data, it was just a question of analysing it and reporting the results. I was also fortunate that every weekend Fiona insisted that we get our boots on and head out onto the mountains, which probably kept me sane. However, I did actually manage to submit my thesis before the fellowship ended. After a really nervous start, the defence of the thesis went well. Indeed, the only changes I needed to make was one word that I had typed wrongly – twice. I also submitted a proposal to the Scottish Office for a Senior Research Fellowship to extend my research project and this was granted. So I was now fully funded post-doctoral researcher for another two years. This was 1994 and I had been sober for ten years which led my supervisor's wife to make the lovely quip, that I had gone from 'a drunk to a doctor in a decade'.

It was during this fellowship that I became interested in the use of computers in a therapeutic situation. I wanted to test out my measurement tool and motivational enhancement treatment that it facilitated in a real-life alcohol treatment setting. Since it was going to be very difficult to train therapists to apply the treatment uniformly, I decided to deliver the treatment by computer. So, accidentally I managed to carry out the first computer assisted alcohol treatment program in the world. Something that I would return to in later years.

Although I was still enjoying the research, I was a bit conflicted on the direction to take my work. Part of me wanted to develop its theoretical base, which would have entailed me focussing more on general psychological principles and less on addiction. However, our work and publications had drawn the attention of a couple of heavyweights in the addiction field. They influenced Barry to direct my work into the treatment arena and he saw an opening into the upper echelon of the world of addiction research. So reluctantly this was the direction we took and, admittedly it was rather successful. But I often think about where the work might have gone, if I had been left to my own devices; who knows, maybe it would have gone nowhere!

Having tasted the academic world, I decided that this was where I wanted my future to lie. My fellowship was coming to an end and I needed to think what to do for a job. I could apply for more grants, and since I was building a reputation there was a good chance that I would be successful. But what I really wanted was to have the security of a permanent post as a lecturer. At the time two lecturer posts were about to become available in the psychology department of Glasgow University. A chat with the head of department suggested that I was a likely candidate for one of them. However, as it turned out I never even got the opportunity to apply, as deals were done behind closed doors. It is almost certain that these internal political manoeuvrings would be illegal today, but hey, that was a different time and different rules.

As luck would have it, the University of Paisley were about to advertise two lectureships, one in the psychology department and the other in the Centre for Alcohol and Drug Studies (CADS). I applied for both and was interviewed for both. CADS was very well known in the addiction field, especially in Scotland. Some very well-known researchers had worked there, so it had a very good reputation. When I went for the interview, I loved the place. The department shared a large house that had been gifted to the university by James Robertson, who had owned a very successful jam and marmalade company. It sat in its own grounds and was completely self-contained. The lecture theatre had a wonderful barrel ceiling and leaded windows and French doors leading out to the garden. There was just a lovely laid-back atmosphere to the place.

Fortunately, I was awarded the lectureship, not only that, I received a pay rise and, best of all, was given tenure. At a time when many university contracts tended to be temporary, e.g. two years, tenure was both rare and very important. It meant that, short of gross misconduct, or the university going bust, the faculty member had a job for life. It was used at one time to protect academic freedom, something which feels more precarious now than it was then.

The early years at CADS were enjoyable for me. There was a great team of around ten including a couple of researchers, three trainers a couple of secretaries, the director Ken and myself. This meant that Ken and I did all the teaching, and it was a lot: twelve weeks of five days, 9am to 5pm. Although, there were only 12 to 16 students, this was not a teaching load that I was used to. And I can't say there was a lot of guidance regarding the subject matter at the outset. Ken handed me a pile of handwritten slides for the overhead projector and said, "Go and teach that." By the second year I had sorted it out and made all my own slides, notes and curriculum.

Ken had an interesting, and rather frustrating, management style. If you had a suggestion, he always sounded interested, and never said no. It took me a while to realise that this was part of his way of avoiding confrontation or disappointment. However, nothing actually changed. The proposal would just sit on his desk forever as part of the ever growing pile of things that he had not 'said no' to. It was difficult to get anything to change. The course in CADS ran on a different timescale to all the other courses in the university, which was one of the reasons for the low student numbers. Most of them were mature students who worked in the alcohol, social work or prison fields. Historically these are organisations that tend to be understaffed and underfunded. The staff needed to be seconded to attend the course, which would take a significant chunk of the training budget for most of these organisations. Also it was the only course of its type in Scotland but was very expensive for anyone to attend if they did not live locally. Two things happened to allow me to change the course and its delivery.

The first was an invitation to write an undergraduate course on Research Methods for Hong Kong University. Paisley University had a new department producing distance learning materials, mostly for internal use, but some for other universities. When the contract to produce courses for Hong Kong University was secured, the head of this new department asked me if I would write the course. I immediately said yes, as I thought that it would be a new challenge and it was a good opportunity to pick up some new skills. Plus, as it was not part of my duties, they were actually going to pay me for it.

Working with the technical writers was an interesting experience. My lecturing and teaching skills had improved immensely over the past few years. Indeed, the feedback from the students, both formal and informal, was consistently excellent. However, writing the course for distance learners I believe helped my teaching practice. When I taught, I was happy to take questions, repeat information from a different viewpoint and loop back to previous lessons when required. But, since distance learning students do not have the benefits of having the teacher present when they read the course, all the information must be both available and in the required order. This forced me to think about these lessons from a student's perspective and become more organised and structured in my writing. The technical writers also helped me with this greatly.

While producing the materials for Hong Kong, I could not help thinking that we should be providing a distance learning option for our own students. The cost of attending the course would be much reduced and the students would not have to negotiate a three-month secondment. Many of the prospective students found the secondment difficult, if not impossible, to obtain as often they worked in small departments that could not afford to have one member of staff to be away for a prolonged period. When I mentioned this to Ken I got the usual reaction, basically a 'not no'. But by now I knew that this meant that nothing would happen.

The second thing to happen was that Ken took an extended period of time off work to have an operation. He had a congenital hip deformity that was increasingly causing him pain when walking, and he had a date for corrective surgery. So, since he was going to be absent for a few months, leaving me as acting director of CADS, I thought that I would take the opportunity to introduce some of the changes I had been advocating for ages. After getting the go ahead from the Dean of School, I started the task of producing the distance learning materials for the course. This was quite a large undertaking as there were four modules: Understanding Alcohol and Drug Use, Theories of Behaviour Change, Research Methods and Practice Placement. There were the logistics involved in changing the timing of the course to fit the semester system used by the rest of the university. However, the rest of the staff were very supportive of these changes, and the students could also see that there was a benefit. Once the changes were underway and it was a *fait accompli,* I visited Ken at home, took him a card, some grapes and the news that

I had changed the course in his absence. Although I expected more of a reaction, he seemed quite pragmatic about it. Maybe he saw that there were benefits and he did not actually have to do the work to reap the rewards. One of the undoubted benefits was that the student numbers increased immediately from 12-16 per year to 50-60, and this increase in numbers and fees made the university happy. It also made us the biggest postgraduate course on alcohol and drugs in the UK, which gave the university some bragging rights.

The other goal that I managed to accomplish in Ken's absence was to persuade the university to finance an international conference. This was the first addiction conference to be held at the University for many years and the first ever of the scale that we achieved. I talked to Paisley Town Council about using some of the historic buildings to host some of the social events. They were more than happy to support us as it was very good publicity for the town. So they permitted us to use the museum for lunches, which allowed our guests, particular the international ones, to find out about Paisley and the mills that manufactured the cloth with the famous Paisley pattern. They also gave us the town hall to host a civic reception, which they paid for, followed by a Ceilidh, which all the guests loved. Although I was a bit concerned that we were going to lose one of the American professors through over exertion when dancing the 'Strip the Willow'. The conference was highly successful financially and also from a PR point of view. So, I repeated the event twice more while I was at the university. Both the students and the staff loved the conferences, as there was a real buzz about the department during these events. Also, it gave them the opportunity to meet and talk with some of the names that they had read about in their course.

While at Paisley I became very active in the addiction research/treatment community. For four years I was the Chairperson of the Scottish Council on Alcohol Therapist Training Courses and Research Consultant to the Board. Following that I became the Research Consultant to the Board of the Renfrewshire Council on Alcohol. During that time I was fortunate enough to obtain a number of research grants and published widely in prestigious journals and contributed chapters to some books. A couple of journals appointed me as a reviewer for submitted papers, which was an honour as it demonstrated their faith in my analytical abilities. I was also appointed external examiner to the addiction courses in Southampton and Bournemouth Universities.

A part of the work that I enjoyed most was working directly on an individual basis with students. As part of the restructuring of the CADS course, I introduced an optional final dissertation where students could elevate their qualification from a Diploma to a Master's degree. So part of my role was to be research supervisor to these students and help them achieve their goals. At the same time I also provided supervision to some PhD students. A challenge that I really enjoyed, as it stretched me to work with these future academics.

One of my last achievements before leaving Paisley was forging a partnership with the Renfrewshire Council on Alcohol (RCA). There was a presentation at the university where I discovered that there was an initiative called a Knowledge Transfer Partnership (KTP) where the university would forge a partnership with a business bringing some expertise to that business. The government would provide the funding for a member of staff who would liaise between the university and industry. Mostly these KTPs were in the field of business or science. However, I saw a possible opportunity to do something different by researching best, most effective practice in addiction treatment, package it into courses and sell it in the form of training to other organisations. So we were funded to the tune of £250,000. As it transpired, this was the first time that the KTP had been used in this way. So ours was the first time there had been an award made to a school of social science. Further, the head of the initiative came over and told me that it had been discussed in 10 Downing Street. Although he never actually told us who discussed it, who knows, maybe it was the gardener. Unfortunately, I left the university before the completion of the project. But before I left, it was amusing to watch the scramble to take ownership of this prestigious project. The issue was finally resolved by someone who previously had nothing to do with the project playing the seniority card. So the project was grabbed by the person with highest status, rather than someone who was more suitable to steer it to its potential. No change there. I never did find out what happened with it after I left.

15: Sheila

Sheila came into my life when Fiona and I had been separated for about five months, and after it had become obvious that there was not going to be any reconciliation. Like me, she worked in Paisley, although she worked for the NHS as a Consultant in Public Health.

Initially things did not get off to a great start. We went out in a date one night, a curry on Byers Road, but it was not a great success! There seemed to be too many things she did not like about me, in particular that I smoked. So after the meal and a drink, we decided to go our separate ways.

A week or so later I was surprised to receive a phone call at work from Sheila. Would I drop round and see her later that night, she needed to talk to someone and, despite all the things that she was not sure about me, she thought that I was good listener. It appeared that her estranged husband had been in touch, and she was considering getting back together with him. She knew in her heart that it was a bad idea, but she was tired of living alone. That night she just needed to be able to talk, mainly to herself, about all the pros and cons of going back into a relationship that had not been happy, for either of them. So I sat and listened and then we had supper and I went home.

After that we started what I felt was a casual friendship, albeit one with benefits, as I was not yet ready for a relationship at that time. However, after going out for a couple of weeks, Sheila suddenly declared that she was in love with me, a revelation that almost finished the relationship before it started. I was not emotionally in a place where I could commit to any relationship, and I said so. Sheila said that although she was a bit disappointed, she was happy to slow things down and take it a bit more casually.

A couple of months into the relationship, I was due to go to Cape Town, to a conference on addiction. Rather unexpectedly, Sheila suggested that she should come with me. It seemed like a nice idea, I was happy to have a travelling companion, since otherwise I was going on my own. So we decided that since she was coming then we should extend our visit and see some of the country. Off we went with very little planned, apart from flights and accommodation for the first couple of nights and for the conference. The remainder of our time there was open to whatever we would decide while we were there.

Before our visit, there had been many reports of unrest in South Africa and warnings to tourists about safety. After a day talking about whether we should hire a car and tour, we decided to go for it, this may be our only chance to see some of this wonderful country. So, off we went down the famous Garden Route, a beautiful 500 mile drive along the coast to Port Elizabeth. Our first stop was in a little seaside town called Hermanus where, completely unknown to us, the Whale Festival was in full swing. This was the time of the year when southern right whales and humpback whales came to that bay to calf. The sight that greeted us was a bay full of whales and their babies. It was absolutely breathtaking. Nobody needed to take a boat to see them. In fact one the restaurants (*Bientang's Cave* I think it was called) had decking out into the bay, which meant that you could have dinner with whales no more than a few feet from your table. We had dinner there but I have no idea what the food was like, although I do know it was expensive. But it wasn't the food you were paying for, it was the experience of being so close to these wonderful creatures and their newborn calves.

We stopped at a number of places along the route and returned back through the hinterland through mountains and endless plains. It was an amazing couple of weeks but I had one bucket list item that I wanted to achieve, which was one of the only things I had planned before leaving Scotland. It was my ambition to dive with great white sharks, and I managed to achieve that at a place called Gansbaai. It was an awesome experience to be in this very flimsy cage (I had thought that the cage would have steel bars, this one had what looked like chicken wire wrapped around four posts) as three huge great white sharks circled it, presumably wondering what I would taste like. While they are magnificent animals, looking directly into their eyes is chilling. With the whales, there had been a spark of recognition (maybe even more than a spark) but with the sharks, nothing, absolutely nothing! When I climbed out the cage, the alpha male actually attacked the cage and took a bite out of it. Fortunately I had only just made it back to the boat by that time.

I loved the thrill of being in the water with these awesome creatures, but I doubt if I would do it again. Not through fear, it was exciting and the potential danger was definitely part of the thrill. But I have concerns about the safety of future tourists, as it definitely felt like safety was a secondary consideration to enterprise. I also fear for the sharks, as the cage diving industry, by very definition, encourages sharks to come closer to humans. If there are accidents, then the sharks could pay the penalty by being hunted again. That would be sad. The hypocrisy of my position, I've done it, so now you can stop, has not escaped me in the least. In my defence sometimes we need to experience a practice to realise the associated problems. I believe this is a case in point – well, that's my excuse anyway.

Sheila loved status. She loved to be important, even to be important by association. One of the things she loved about the conference in Cape Town, was that she discovered that I was actually rather well known in the addiction field. She enjoyed that I could introduce her to all the main speakers and organisers of the conference, and that they all knew me and my work. This came as a pleasant surprise to her, and she regarded me in a new light after that.

After returning from the conference, we settled into a steady relationship and spent our time between Sheila's flat in the west end of Glasgow, my house in Chapelton and my caravan in Inveraray. This was a very different relationship from the one I had with Fiona. For a start Sheila had a daughter, Vicky, which brought a very different dynamic. It thrust me into a parental role that I was not sure I either wanted, or was equipped for. Vicky was a lovely girl who had suffered a diabetic seizure in infancy, which had left her with a slight limp and also minor learning difficulties. She did not live with us for long, as her father helped her to buy a flat in the next street to Sheila. Vicky's father was Greek and lived in Athens. He was an eye surgeon with his own practice there. So, buying a flat for Vicky had a double benefit, it helped her to become independent and gave him somewhere to stay when he came to Scotland to visit her.

Another difference was that, as a consultant, Sheila had a considerably larger salary than Fiona had, and larger than mine also. So, it was much easier to book more expensive holidays than I could previously. The first holiday we had was to Hurghada in Egypt. We were going away for the New Year to get a bit of winter sun. However, unfortunately the weather in Scotland was very stormy with lots of heavy snow. This meant that all flights out of Glasgow were considerably delayed till they managed to clear the runway. By the time they managed that our connecting flight from London to Hurghada had gone, and there was only one flight a week. When we contacted the travel company, they told us that if we could manage to get to Luxor, they would get us accommodation on a Nile cruise boat, and then they would transport us to Hurghada.

As it turned out, this delay was a blessing in disguise. We flew to Luxor and a guide picked us up from the airport and transported us to the cruise ship. When the travel company had said that we would be dining on the Nile that evening, I had imagined something a bit more upmarket. When we arrived at the dock, we saw all these absolutely beautiful boats all lined up side by side. To get to our ship we had to walk across all of these wonderful, luxurious boats to get to ours, which looked more like a working barge. This cruise ship was full of Belgian tourists who looked as if they were passengers on a slave ship, rather than having a beautiful cruise. And as for the boat, I've probably dived on better wrecks. However, it was only for one night. On the way to the ship, the tour guide suggested that we could use this detour to our advantage with a visit to the Temple of Karnak in the morning, and in the afternoon he would take us to the Valley of the Kings. So, we had the bonus of crossing the Nile on a traditional sailing felucca and visiting the tombs of Rameses II and Tutankhamun. None of which would have been possible without the snow.

The next day we travelled to Hurghada in a luxurious private minibus, just the two of us and the driver. To get there we had to drive across the Arabian desert, a wild and barren place. Because of the threat of terrorists and bandits, we had to travel in a convoy escorted by armed police. This was a rather thrilling and, at times, scary journey as the Arab drivers raced each other, and played chicken with oncoming traffic.

We were in a beautiful resort on the shores of the Red Sea, one of the most popular diving areas of the world. I was very much looking forward to diving there, but Sheila had a fear of even putting her face in the water. Nevertheless I managed to persuade her to snorkel with me to a nearby tiny reef which had masses of fish, and she really enjoyed it. So, despite her fear, she signed up to learn to dive, which I thought was an incredibly brave thing to do and I was touched by her gift. On her final dive of the course, the instructor allowed me to dive with her, and we swam together through a beautiful coral garden, surrounded by shoals of angel fish. On the boat journey back to the hotel a huge pod of dolphins came and played alongside the boat. It felt that they had come to welcome the new diver as a fellow marine being. However, although she had passed her course, this was the only dive we would ever have together.

We had booked to dive together in the Turks and Caicos, but on the first outing the sea was so rough that almost everyone was seasick and many of the group decided against diving that day. I dived anyway and continued to do so on subsequent days of the holiday, as well as on later trips when we went to the Caribbean,

Adriatic and Mediterranean. I was disappointed that we did not dive together again, but I was also philosophical. Scuba diving is not a sport that everyone enjoys, some people become very claustrophobic and/or anxious. I was impressed that she had overcome her fears, and flattered that she had done it to please me. And I understood that she had not enjoyed it as much as I would have liked, or even enough to want to continue.

After we had been together for about 18 months, my house in Chapelton finally sold and I moved into Sheila's Glasgow flat. I had already been living with her most of the time anyway, the only difference was I now had nowhere that was mine. So we decided to buy a 'holiday' home, or that was how we thought about it then. Initially we thought that this would be my property but Sheila decided that, so that she could feel a bit of ownership, she wanted to have a share, so we decided on 20% would be Sheila's with the rest being mine. We looked all around our favourite areas in Argyle where the caravan was, I sold this also, as the new place would replace it. Eventually, I found a wonderful place at the end of the Rosneath peninsula in the village of Kilcreggan. It was the whole ground floor of a large detached Victorian house set in an acre of garden with the most spectacular 180 degree view of the Clyde estuary. I loved that house, and everyone who visited also fell in love with it.

Around this time, the post of Director of Public Health for the Western Isles became available. I strongly advocated for Sheila to apply for the post. She was ambitious and there were very few comparable posts in Scotland, so I believed that this would be good for her. Of course, I also thought that she would be good in the post as well. Sheila applied and got the job, which came with a house in Stornoway. Now we were spending our time between three houses, Glasgow, Kilcreggan and whenever I could be free, Stornoway. Sheila spent most of the week in Stornoway and came back to Glasgow at weekends. I would work from Glasgow and we would often spend weekends in Kilcreggan. After a while, I moved down to Kilcreggan and commuted from there, which caused a bit of friction between us. However, I could not see the point of living in the Glasgow flat when she was in Stornoway. I told her that I'm not a city boy, I'm much more at home in small towns and the country. Reluctantly she accepted that.

The Western Isles became one of my favourite places, still is. Maria, my cousin, had moved there to marry a local about sixteen years before and my regular visits there brought us closer. In fact for the next few years we spent most Easter Sundays together at their home in the village of Arnol, on the west side of the Isle of Lewis. I fell very much in love with the Western Isles, the wild bleakness contrasting with the stunning beaches and, one of the real attractions for me, the emptiness of the place. At one time we discussed actually making this our home, and Sheila talked about us getting married in Stornoway. I really didn't want to get married, as I felt that the relationship was a bit too volatile and I did not want either, or both of us, to get hurt again. I did consider moving to Stornoway permanently though. In fact I had a meeting with the principal of the University of the Highlands and Islands UHI) to discuss a lecturer post. At Paisley University I had been heavily involved in distance learning and moving our classroom-based course to a blended on (online and/or face to face) and this experience, plus my research record, was very interesting to the UHI. They seemed keen to have me, but they did not have the money to fund a new post, but would have been willing to look at possible sources of funding. Since I had tenure at Paisley, moving to UHI to a post that had short-term funding would have been a risk, a risk that I would have been unwilling to take at that time. Maybe if our relationship had been more solid, I would have been more motivated to take the chance.

Our backgrounds were very different. Sheila came from a large family, three sisters and two brothers, whereas I was brought up as an only child. Her family was wealthy and successful, her father had been the managing director of a very large whisky business, as well as being the chairman of the board for the Scottish Whisky Industry. One brother was senior management in a printing firm, while the other was a stockbroker and investment consultant in Hong Kong. Sheila was the only sister to actually work, as the others had all married well. She grew up in a large detached private house and I grew up in a council house. So very different experiences. She would, jokingly I think, describe me as her 'bit of rough'.

Sheila introduced me to a more expansive lifestyle. Growing up in the working class can limit one's horizons. This is most definitely not inevitable and the cultural changes of the 60s went a long way to sweep away many of these limitations, but not completely However, these limitations are not actually about social class or even opportunity, they tend to be more about attitude and example. One instance of this is opera. I don't know anyone from my social circle who had ever been to see an opera, whereas when I met Sheila and her friends, almost all of whom were professional people such as lawyers, doctors and bankers, they all had an annual season ticket to the opera and considered it to be a normal activity. Fortunately, I was very open to new experiences, even opera. In fact, I have always had a love of music and have a very eclectic taste in music, so there was plenty of space in my life for this new experience. The first opera we went to was

Salome. Unfortunately it was sung in German, not the most musical of languages, so I was a bit unsure about whether I wanted to go again. However, we went to other, more lyrical operas and by the bye I grew to love opera and still listen to it regularly.

Our life was interesting. Sheila worked mostly in Stornoway and I worked between home and the university. Sometimes I would have a day where I would invite my research students to come to my house in Kilcreggan, where we could work without the distractions and demands of the rest of the department. When she came back at weekends, we often entertained either in Glasgow or Kilcreggan and during holidays I would spend extended periods in the Western Isles. Coupled with great holidays, a stay in Venice, sailing in a flotilla round Greece and going to the Olympic Games in Athens, life for us was, at least externally, good.

One definite fly in the ointment was the fact that we tended to argue, a lot and quite savagely. We broke up many times, but they never lasted too long. One of us would phone and then we would find ourselves wondering what it was that we had been arguing about. Obviously, since this is my story, I would like to blame Sheila for the arguments. But that would almost certainly be untrue. Yes, Sheila could be imperious, controlling and unreasonable, that I'm not going to deny. But I was stubborn, had a super-sensitivity to being controlled, and could manage to find an insult in the most lavish of compliments. We could both be loving and generous, Sheila could be extremely generous, and we both admired and liked each other. However, the arguments got more frequent and the breakups became longer. I promised myself many times that this was definitely the last time, I did not want to continue to live like this. The weekdays when Sheila was in Stornoway tended to be peaceful, we would phone each other in the evening and that was OK. When she returned at the weekend, we often did not manage to get through the whole weekend without some argument.

The crunch came on a holiday to Slovenia. We had had a lovely time up in the Alpine region at Lake Bled and then moved to a seaside town, Koper, for the remainder of the holiday. We decided to go for a walk along the coastal path and then Sheila suddenly decided that we should go in a different direction. Everything boiled over, the last couple of years of arguing then making up all just came pouring out, and there we were in the middle of the street in this otherwise peaceful little town, screaming at each other. That day I decided that I could not continue with this relationship. It was unhealthy for both of us. We did manage to talk to each other, and later she asked me to go to a family party in Edinburgh, to which I agreed, but the reality was that our relationship died that day in Koper.

As described at the start of this book, I had written to Lou for no specific reason that I could think of. Then Lou had phoned me. Sheila had been with me in Kilcreggan when Lou phoned. She was actually leaving to go back to Glasgow and get changed and I was to pick her up to travel through to Edinburgh. So she left just about a couple of minutes into the phone call. When she got back to her flat, she phoned up and asked me who had phoned. When I told her, she lost her temper and started screaming at me about being unfaithful to her. I totally denied this, but she just said that she did not want me to go to Edinburgh with her and slammed the phone down.

A couple of days later she phoned demanding an apology and also demanding to know why I had betrayed her. When I tried to explain the situation she refused to listen; we were at an impasse. A large part of me was relieved. I had no designs, honourable or otherwise, towards Lou at that time. However, I knew that my relationship with Sheila had become toxic and it needed to end. Since we had 'ended' it unsuccessfully many times in the past, maybe this was the only way we could break free, with a huge row.

Nothing happened with Sheila or Lou in the next few weeks. The silence between Sheila and I was deafening. Lou, as arranged, phoned again two weeks later and weekly thereafter. When it was decided that I would sell the Kilcreggan house, move to Devon and marry Lou, Sheila refused to allow the house to be sold. She owned 20% of the property and her permission was required for a sale. To me it seemed like a pointless and rather petty gesture, but for a couple of months she was adamant. Eventually she reneged and allowed the house to be sold.

Months later I went to say goodbye to her, as I was leaving to go to Devon and marry Lou. The meeting was a poignant one, parting from someone you shared a significant part of your life (seven years) almost always is. Sheila admitted that she had handled the situation badly, which was quite a big step for her. She said that she felt that her behaviour had actually driven me into Lou's arms. I'm not sure whether that was true or not. Personally, I believe that Lou and I were meant to be together and that it would have happened regardless of Sheila's behaviour. But, yes, it certainly made it easier for Lou and I to be together.

We only spoke once after that meeting. Sheila said that she had phoned me by accident. I was not convinced, as she seemed very keen to tell me that she was engaged to a professor from Strathclyde University in Glasgow. I said I was glad for her, and I really meant it. I never heard whether she had actually married him or not. A couple of years later I got a call from my cousin Maria to tell me that Sheila had died of a heart attack That made me sad.

I have some very good memories of Sheila, she could be a lot of fun and she said that I made her laugh more than anyone else (I assume that was a compliment and not a veiled insult). And when we were good, we made a great couple. Unfortunately, the arguments were too frequent, and sometimes too hurtful, to sustain a healthy relationship. RIP Sheila!

16: If Conclusion Jumping was an Olympic Sport ...

A few years before my breakup with Sheila, my mother was in hospital and facing death. She had been unwell with heart problems for many years, in fact she had a triple by-pass about twenty years before this, and had been told then that her life expectancy was another ten years. But now, as well as the heart issue, she had cancer of the oesophagus. The lesions in her throat would periodically bleed, and she would be rushed into hospital. These bleeds were a medical emergency as any one of them could end her life.

At the time, the surgeon told me that he could surgically remove the tumours relatively easily, but her heart condition made it unlikely she would survive the operation. The doctors were advising that her prognosis was not very good, suggesting that she probably did not have much time. Because of the uncertainty of her illness, Sheila and I decided to holiday at home that year (2003). We felt that we needed to be available to get to the hospital very quickly if needed.

I decided that we should try something different, so I booked a hotel on the Ardnamurchan peninsula. It is no exaggeration to say that this a rather remote and sparsely populated area of Scotland. It is known, although not very widely known, for its beauty. To give some perspective of its remoteness, a couple of years ago a TV company filmed a series, where a group of people had to survive in the wilderness. They filmed this series in Ardnamurchan, nearly twenty years after we were there!

After a journey along winding single-track roads, we arrived at the Kilchoan Hotel mid afternoon and parked the car at the rear of the hotel. As we got out of the car, we saw a door and wandered in. The door was actually the staff entrance and took us into storage areas, which looked generally chaotic. Sheila, having endured the drive through (for me beautiful unspoilt countryside, for her a deserted wilderness) was already less than enthusiastic about going to the back end of nowhere. Now she decided that there was no way that she was going to stay in this run-down, cheerless and isolated place. Indeed, she was adamant that nothing would induce her to stay there and, what on earth was I thinking about, bringing her to a place like this. So off we went to see if we could find an acceptable place to stay for a few nights.

Fortunately we found a nice bed and breakfast place, with a large double room which had a beautiful sea view toward the Isle of Mull. After we dumped our luggage and settled in, it was time to think about eating. Our hostess informed us that the only place that served food in the evening was, you guessed it, the Kilchoan Hotel. So, of necessity and with no other choice, we made our way back to the hotel.

This time we entered by the front door and asked at reception if they had a table for dinner. She called someone from the lounge who took us through to a lovely, comfortable dining room. In fact the whole hotel looked very nice indeed, exactly what you would expect and want a country hotel to be. And, as it turned out, the food was excellent as well. At least Sheila had the good grace to look a bit embarrassed about her earlier Olympic-class conclusion jumping.

While it is easy to become very smug about her presumption, and I did; she is not alone in jumping to conclusions prior to proper investigation – many, if not most, people do it. Some psychologists label this tendency to make decisions, based on scanty and inadequate information as a 'cognitive distortion'. It is in fact a short cut we use to prevent us being overwhelmed by the huge amount of information that we receive on a day-to-day basis. So it is a useful method the brain uses to streamline processing. However, there are times when it is not very helpful, as bias and prejudice become the main factors that we use to make decisions. Unsurprisingly, at times like that, we often make the wrong decisions, whether we are aware of it, or, perhaps more to the point, would actually admit it.

At many points in my existence I have searched for the meaning of life, both mine and everyone else's. The search has taken me to a seminary to train for the priesthood. It has taken me to an ashram to sit at the feet of Guru Maharaj Ji. It took me into books of eastern philosophy or of other religions and it took me to a Christian commune in Devon. My descent into alcohol and drugs, in particular psychedelic drugs, was just a somewhat distorted way of trying to find out who I was, and where I fitted in the world. Finally, reluctantly the twelve-step programme of Alcoholics Anonymous helped answer some of those questions and brought God back into my life. Just not too close please! Now that Lou and I were getting close, I knew that she would want to know where I stood on Christianity. The answer to that was complicated. On the one hand, I had never really stopped believing in God. True, my view of him often changed. Sometimes I saw him as a benevolent God who loved mankind, and other times I saw him as more in the guise of the God of the Old Testament, all judging and smiting. Mostly, I was OK with the relationship that God and I had. It felt like we were neighbours living next to each other. I was slightly aware of him coming and going but, there was an unspoken agreement that we would never actually meet in the hallway. That would just have been too embarrassing.

We did kind of communicate. If you asked me, "Do you pray?" I would have said yes, sometimes. What I meant by that was that I would send off a quick "God help me!" when I felt the need, usually when I felt in trouble. But, in keeping with our unspoken agreement, it was analogous to leaving a message on God's answering machine or a letter to Father Christmas. I was certainly not looking for a situation where I called and then heard a voice saying, "Hi John, your call has been put straight through to God here, how can I help?" No, having God around, but in the background was comforting, and the height of my ambition in this regard.

In truth, my problem was not really with God. My problem was really twofold. Firstly, I had a problem with religion. To clarify, by religion I mean the rules that surround belief in God, whether they are man's interpretation of God's wishes, or man's assumptions about how to behave. For much of my life I had not really been a 'joiner'. Being part of a group, a gang or a congregation had not been high on my list. Indeed, I tended to avoid it wherever possible, particularly when the membership was accompanied by lots of formal rules. And let's face it, most religions have lots of rules and, if we are really honest, most of them having very little to do with God.

Over the last few decades, it feels like the attitudes and morals of religion versus secular life have diverged markedly, at least in public. Personally, I have always been quite liberal in my beliefs.

Partly that was my socialist upbringing, partly my hippy leanings. So, I have always struggled with the more fundamentalist elements of religion, and any other group. This was just as true, even at my most devout periods. The 'fear preaching' of the White Fathers was repellent to me, as is the messages emerging from some of the more famous, or should that be infamous, churches in the USA who practice their own version of vitriolic preaching.

Secular society by contrast, presents a vision of personal freedom and respect which, superficially, sounds enlightened and appealing. However, if you dare to question the current orthodoxy, the secular version of the White Fathers quickly emerges, armed with the modern-day equivalent of the Spanish Inquisition. Instead of torture in some subterranean dungeon in order to make the heretics recant, it is now done in the searing light of social media. Careers can be destroyed, as the shadowy anonymous critics take to Twitter (now 'X') to point out the errors in someone's thinking and to decide on their 'worthiness' to be heard, hold a job, or be part of the 'right thinking' and 'kind' community (or should that be congregation). The Spanish Inquisition might have broken your body, but at least if you recanted you would be deemed to be saved, today's equivalent is much less forgiving. Of course these are the extremes: not all Christians are fundamentalists and not all non-Christians are rabid Twitter assassins. There is middle ground, although sometimes it seems like a very narrow strip, more of a tightrope.

The second issue I had about embracing Christianity again, was me. My past record with religion had never been as a moderate. As I have written above, my searching led me not just to merely observe the laws of Catholicism, like for example my parents had: instead, I had to become the priest. It was not enough to read about eastern mysticism, I needed to move into the Ashram. And I was not content with becoming a Christian, I needed to move into the community and apply to Bible college. With this sort of extremist history, I was wary about letting this overzealous, almost obsessional, part of me loose again. I was afraid that I would become a narrow-minded bigot, at odds with all around me.

This oppressive view of Christianity was reinforced by attitudes at the university where I worked, and most other universities at that time. Being a Christian was regarded as anti-intellectual! This was the last thing that I as a lecturer, and an insecure one at that, would want. And, in truth I had also bought into this belief, even though I still kept the emergency prayer line open to God. I did that in secret. So, I suppose my answer to Lou's impending question was that I was a liberal, left of centre, undercover agnostic (most days, if there was not an emergency, I was more hopeful than agnostic). Sorry, but I did say that it was complicated.

So, basically my fears were that, if I were to become a Christian again, I would instantly turn into a rabid, narrow-minded bigot, standing on street corners waving a placard with the word 'REPENT'; and that I would dive into this intolerant, judgmental persona totally and irrevocably. After all if I was going to be a bigot, then my history suggested that I would probably try to be the best bigot I could possibly be, with the result that everyone who knew me would justifiably shun me. I was fairly confident that this was probably not the answer that Lou would want to hear.

My dilemma was that I did love her; maybe I could just go to church with her and pretend that I believed everything she believed. But I also had my integrity, plus I am a hopeless liar, I just do not have the required poker face to pull it off. As I discussed earlier, I was a useless salesman. Where did this leave me, or her?

For one thing, when I looked at Lou, I knew she was a Christian, and quite a devout one. But, somewhat puzzlingly, she did not seem to demonstrate any obvious symptoms of narrow mindedness or rampant bigotry. In fact she seemed almost normal. She was clearly intelligent. She was very kind and loving. If I did not know better, I would have said that she could not possibly be a Christian. I tried to comfort myself with the belief that the narrow-mindedness and bigotry may not be compulsory for membership. Maybe there was a branch of Christianity where you could pick and choose your prejudices. That seemed like a possible loophole for me. Maybe I could become a Christian without having to condemn all the usual suspects, such as gay people.

At that time, the irony was completely lost on me. I did not realise that I had already become the thing that I feared. I was the narrow-minded bigot. I was the world class conclusion jumper. The only difference was that my self-righteousness was critical and condemnatory of Christians, rather than other groups. Didn't Jesus say something about pointing out the motes in others' eyes while missing the plank in our own (never been sure what a mote is, assume it must be some speck of dust–otherwise the analogy doesn't work). I think I had a whole forest in there.

If our relationship was going to happen at all, one of us was going to need to change or, at least, compromise. I could not see Lou being the one to change. She had been a committed Christian for most of her life and had exercised, until relatively recently, a ministry of evangelism. She would give concerts, where she performed her music and talked about God. So her changing to suit me was not something that I expected was going to happen, neither did I want that to happen. I dearly wanted her to be who she was, and the person I loved, and not change to suit me and perhaps turn into someone less loveable.

If this relationship was going to develop and flourish, the question was, could I become more open minded and also conquer my fear of my excess? A big question, or is that two big questions.

17: An Appointment with God

Many years ago I learned to scuba dive in a Scottish loch (Loch Fyne) in late autumn. The weather was everything that people expect of autumn in Scotland, grey, overcast and not very warm. I looked round my fellow students as they waited to go on their first ever real dive, and they all had a rather forced grin on their faces. Before today, we had only practised diving in a swimming pool, which is a whole lot less scary. Looking back they were all probably equally as scared and exhilarated as I was, but at the time my perception was that they just seemed to be enjoying it much more than I was. I really wanted to get out there and dive, but my mind was full of what ifs, and I'm sure someone close to the shore was playing the theme from Jaws. I could definitely hear it in my mind, very clearly Da Dum, Da Dum!

At last we were ready to go and we swam out into the loch and waited for the instructor to give the signal to dive. Then on cue we all let the air out of our buoyancy jackets, breathed out to empty our lungs and slowly sank into the depths of the loch.

It was scary, exciting and very strange. We were under water in an alien world that was gloomy, eerie, but beautiful. The water had a sepia tinge from the peat washed down from the surrounding mountains. It was a bit like swimming through whisky. Beautiful though it was, this was not our environment and there was a real sense of being a stranger there, but also there was a great sense of privilege at being there, doing and seeing things that few people do and see. After an intense weekend of diving and practising the safety drills, most of us managed to pass the course and qualify as certified divers. By then we were feeling much more at home in a world that, on the one hand, gave a new freedom of weightlessness, but was also limiting as your vision was restricted to about three or four metres.

A few days later I was diving again. But this time, instead of plunging into the cold gloomy depths of Loch Fyne, I jumped off a boat into the Indian ocean in the Maldives. It could not have been more different to Loch Fyne. The weather was warm, in fact it was very hot, the sun was shining brightly, the water was beautifully warm and clear. This clarity of the water was the most amazing difference. Instead of seeing only a few feet in front of you there were these incredible underwater vistas. As we descended, I felt that I was dropping into a lovely steep canyon full of fish, stingrays and even sharks. It was incredible. In the bar that evening one of the other divers said that she could not take her eyes off my face during that dive, as there was a childlike wonder written all over it. For me that first dive in the Maldives is an experience that will live with me forever. It was just so beyond my previous experience, a moment of sheer joy and exhilaration at being admitted to a new, exciting and beautiful world.

So why am I talking about scuba diving? Because, for me, meeting God was a similar experience, full of fear and excitement and way beyond my previous experience. It was like being taken out of Loch Fyne, with its limited visibility and plunging into a fabulous canyon of light, joy, incredible possibilities and, amazingly, feeling at home.

As you hopefully remember from about half a book ago, Lou and I had met up again after 35 years. After our initial meeting we phoned each other every night, sometimes for about two hours. Lou also came up to Scotland twice to visit, one time bringing her daughter Cassia, and I travelled down to Exeter a few times to see her. On one of these trips, we visited her mother who had been housebound through ill health for around five years. Somehow, at the end of that meeting and on the journey back to Lou's house we decided we were going to get married. We have discussed this on numerous occasions since, and we are convinced of two things. One, Lou did not ask me to marry her and two, I did not ask Lou to marry me. But somehow it was now a fact that we were getting married, and that quite soon.

After all the euphoria had worn off and I was safely back in Scotland, Lou started to have second, third and fourth thoughts. She was a live practising Christian and this was very important to her. Indeed, marrying a non-believer would be a problem for her. She was clear that she loved me, and equally clear that she dearly wanted to marry me. However if I was not a Christian, it would make things difficult. I could understand how important this was to her, she dearly wanted a life partner, a fellow traveller and she understandably doubted her ability to give herself to a lesser relationship.

17: An Appointment with God

To crystallise what she wanted, she told me "You need to ask my Father for my hand in marriage". Ignoring the Jane Austen connotations, I had to point out to her that her father had been dead for ten years. "Not that father, I meant my Father, God". Of course that would be what she meant! But couldn't I just do something a bit more simple instead, like slay a dragon or mount a quest for the golden fleece?

As I have said previously, I have been known to fire off the odd prayer when the occasion demanded it. Over the course of my life, God and I had sometimes been close and sometimes not so close. This was going to be a time when we were going to have to be close. So, resigned to this quest I found myself heading off to find God and ask for his daughter's hand in marriage. Not exactly just another Tuesday.

I have no idea if my experience of meeting God is typical. I suspect it is not, because I believe he meets us all as individuals, but I think that the outcome may be. As I said earlier, Lou had requested that I needed to seek God if our relationship was going to continue. So I set off to find him with very mixed feelings. What if he didn't speak to me, or what was maybe worse, what if he did? I wasn't really sure that I wanted to hear what he would say.

As you have probably gathered by now, I have not exactly lived a blameless life, so the last thing I wanted was to be reminded of all of that, especially by God! It felt a bit like taking my report card home with the comments "John has potential that he is not living up to, he is lazy and wilful, could do better, Grade C-minus." The teachings from my youth of a scary God, and the Hieronymus Bosch paintings of Hell, with the burny fires and demons with pitchforks, all came flooding back to me. However, I had promised to do this, so it was bullet-biting time.

You may be, but probably are not, surprised to hear that I was not a big fan of churches or religion, so when I made the decision to seek God, I decided to go to somewhere where I often felt a spiritual feeling. At the time I lived in Kilcreggan, a lovely little village on the Rosneath Peninsula. If you look at a map of central Scotland it is a lumpy bit sticking out into the Clyde estuary. When I had things to think or pray about, I would go for a walk out to the tip of the peninsula. There is a rocky outcrop there, which is an island at high tide, but can be accessed by a little rocky path when the tide is out. It's a lovely little place which is often the hang out of a seal, which likes to play around that area. The walk there, about a six-mile round trip, is beautiful as it skirts the water's edge, then through a couple of fields and finally through the woods to emerge at the rocky tip, which I later named 'The Cathedral.'

The appointed day was a fairly nondescript kind of day, dry, not especially warm and a bit overcast. I filled my water bottle, made sure my MP3 player was charged up and on shuffle, and then I headed off. Since there was no way of knowing what would happen, I tried to empty my mind of any thoughts or fears about the encounter in front of me and just enjoy the random music that was playing.

After walking for almost an hour I emerged from the woods at the entrance to The Cathedral in fits of giggles. The shuffle on the MP3 player had chosen for this auspicious and solemn moment to play Bob Dylan's *Knocking on Heaven's Door.* Now there's a very fitting entrance, I thought, does this herald what's to come? In hindsight I can say that the answer is an emphatic yes, as fortunately I truly believe that God has a great sense of humour. How else can you account for the fact he loves us?

I walked out onto the little island, switched off the MP3 player, made sure that there was no one around to witness what I was doing, took off my jacket and placed it on a rock, had a drink of water and took a deep breath. As far as I know there is not a little book of etiquette for talking to God (although thinking about it, maybe that's what prayer books, or even the Bible, are for). Anyway, I had no idea what the best way to go about this would be, so I just launched in.

"Well, Lord, I'm here and I guess you know why." I'm not sure what I was expecting to happen next, but I certainly wasn't expecting what then happened.

"I've been waiting for you."

"Eh."

"You have come home."

"Ehhh!!"

I felt a slip in my reality. There was a voice speaking to me, I wasn't sure if it was out loud or in my head, but it was very clear – and it had a distinctly Jewish accent. Just like that first dive in the Maldives, I felt that I had dropped into another world and it was bright, clear and alien. I felt euphoric, I felt warm and tingly, I felt strange and the most incredible part was that somehow this totally weird situation seemed comfortable and normal. It was like being a child in the family home, safe, warm and loved. I'm not sure if my family home had ever felt quite like this, I doubt it, but this was how I wished it had been. If Enid Blyton had designed my family home, this is how it would have been!

My little island had somehow become a little bit of Heaven and the voice that was speaking to me left me in no doubt that I was wanted and loved. I felt like a child on Christmas morning having just opened the best present I could ever have dreamed of.

Tears ran down my face (as I said before, it happens a lot) as I was struck with an incredible poignancy. I had always prided myself on being self-sufficient and independent and yet, as God said "You have come home," I found that there had been a huge ache in my heart to belong. For the first time ever I saw, acknowledged and put down the overwhelming sense of loneliness that I had lived with as my spirit had craved to be united with its God.

God said many things on that island but, unfortunately, I have forgotten most of what he said. You might think it strange that I would forget the detail of the most incredible meeting of my life, but the words were in themselves not that significant. Think of meeting the man or woman of your dreams and looking into their eyes and knowing a sense of overflowing love. You may have a conversation, but the words, even the best-chosen ones, don't mean very much. What does matter and what stays with you is the connection, the feeling of shared love.

That is what that meeting was like; all my senses seemed to be functioning oddly. His words were tasted and felt and his love was seen and heard and I knew, deep in my soul, I just knew, that my heavenly Father was glad that I had come. The big, scary, angry God had not turned up to accuse me. I profoundly knew that I did not deserve his love and that made this meeting and this incredible outcome so much more awesome and special. Standing there immersed in this unconditional love was wonderful. I felt (felt is not the right way to describe it), I knew deep in my being that I was where I should be, and for that instant I was who I should be. I did not want this moment to end, I wanted more, much more. I wanted to stay here forever and yet at the same time I wanted to run home and tell Lou.

How long this 'moment' lasted I have no idea. It seemed to last a very long time and yet there was no sense of time passing. Finally it was time to go back to the house. As I meandered back the way that I had come, I knew that something had fundamentally changed. The world looked different, the woods looked greener, more vital. The sky seemed bluer, brighter, clearer. The estuary seemed even more beautiful than earlier.

Since it is probably safe to say that the world had likely not been totally transformed that afternoon, despite the way it looked, I was left with the conclusion that maybe something had changed in me. What that was and the effect it has had is something we will explore in later chapters.

I am almost certainly as guilty as most people, and even though I have learned over the years, I continue doing it and having to learn the same lessons over and over. That is trying to put God in a box, invent nice little parameters to determine exactly how he works, and maybe even more important, how he doesn't work. This reduces God so that we can understand him on our terms in our time frames. However, God is the great escapologist, continually breaking out of the framework we create for him. Constantly amazing us by how he works. We also do well to break out of 'religion' as it limits our expectations and harms our faith.

Together Again

First, Lou had come to visit me in Scotland so we could spend Valentine's Day together. While she was there, she wanted to see my 'cathedral' where I had gone to meet with God. Unfortunately, it was February in Scotland, which meant that it was cold and wet. So instead of walking the six-mile round trip, we drove as close as we could get to it. All we had to do to get there was a short stroll through some woods to arrive on the beach where we could access the 'cathedral' at low tide. Because of the weather, the short stroll became more of a mad dash to the beach, a quick peak and a repeat dash back to the shelter of the car to escape the downpour.

Back at the car, Lou suggested we have a short prayer of thanks for the 'cathedral' and God having met me there. We settled down to what I expected to be a routine chat with God, with both of us (Lou and me that is) taking turns at saying thanks. We would do this until we had both said all that we wanted to say, and then drive back to my house for a cup of tea and some warmth. It started off that way, but then it took a bit of a turn.

The atmosphere in the car changed quite markedly. Afterwards Lou said that she suddenly became aware of the Holy Spirit being present in the car and she started praying in tongues. She felt that his presence was very strong.

My perception was a tingling sensation that started at my feet and slowly travelled up to encompass my body. Then came the voice, if voice is the right way to describe it, it was soothing. I felt that I was sensing, rather than actually hearing, words. He said "You are not an only child. Your brothers and sister are here".

In my mind, I could see, what I took to be the Holy Spirit with three people slightly younger than me standing smiling at me. They just seemed so glad to see me, and to be seen by me. Then I heard "You are not an only child. These are your siblings and they are excited to meet you."

At that point, something broke inside me and I started sobbing. However, if there is such a thing, it was a good sobbing. My deep existential loneliness and desire for a brother or sister was being healed. I was not an only child; I was not alone. This was a fundamental and profound shift in my self-image. Then I heard "Find a photograph of three people and put it on your screensaver to remind you that you are not alone. You have a family."

During all this Lou was very aware that something significant was happening, deep work was being done. So she just continued to pray and hold me as the Holy Spirit restored my siblings to me in the most amazing and dramatic fashion. Since that day I have never felt as alone as I had done for most of my life.

Tongues

After I had been a professing Christian for some time, people started talking to me about the Baptism of the Spirit. Some people suggested (some stronger than others) that if I was really serious about being a Christian, then I should seek this blessing. It seemed that it would provide me with the spiritual gift of greater union with God, and all the benefits that would bring. I was a bit sceptical about this as I had no desire to speak in tongues.

I had been around enough services and events to encounter a great number of people chattering away incomprehensible phrases. Some sounded like they were speaking a baby form of elfish, others just repeated one or two words over and over. I was happy enough to have greater union with God, but I just did not want the gift of tongues. I could not see any purpose to it, and I felt it made otherwise sensible people look ridiculous. I wanted none of it.

Similar to C.S. Lewis, I have been a reluctant convert. My past record of unquestioning enthusiasm had morphed into an almost ruthless scepticism. However, as I discussed in the previous chapter, I was trying to be more open-minded. So I agreed to investigate what this Baptism of the Spirit was all about.

Off I went to see Gary (our pastor in Exeter). He had very kindly agreed to talk me through what was involved. After discussing it, although I was still sceptical, we decided to pray for the baptism that day. I told him I was willing, just please no tongues!

I asked the Holy Spirit to come and almost immediately I was overcome with a glorious joyful, loving feeling. I laughed a lot, similar to the way I did when I was smoking lots of cannabis. It was a good feeling. I definitely felt the definite presence of God and have since come to recognise his presence. It was a beautiful feeling, and no tongues. I was happy.

A couple of weeks later I was back in Scotland walking along the beach near my house. I stopped at a log, that was almost white from the constant exposure to the elements, where I would often sit and pray. It was a very picturesque and peaceful spot to do that, as it was far enough away from the village so that there was never anyone around. All of a sudden I found myself singing out loud. Not something I normally do, as I am really not a good singer, as many people over the years have told me. But this singing was in tongues! I had no idea what it meant, but there were long, what appeared to be, articulate passages. I started moaning at God. I said I did not want to speak in tongues.

"You didn't, you sang."

"Ooh that was sneaky."

"Yes it was, wasn't it."

Since that day, I have often prayed in tongues. When I do, I feel the presence of God in a much more powerful way. If I really want to feel his presence quickly, I find that I can get myself into a much more receptive place when I speak in tongues. Also, I now realise that using tongues allows the Holy Spirit to pray through me and ask for the things that are important to God rather than my day-to-day concerns. I can honestly say that I am glad to have the gift of tongues and, yes, I was wrong to not want it. So, will I learn to ignore my scepticism in future?

Unfortunately, probably not.

18: Commissioning

One of the things that we enjoyed doing in those early days of our relationship, was to find a nice restaurant and have lunch or dinner. We just enjoyed the relaxed atmosphere of sitting talking, while sampling some nice food and getting to know each other all over again. So, when I visited Exeter, much of our time was spent exploring local eateries. Didn't help the waistlines, but it did help us bond.

On one of my visits we went to lunch at *Dart's Farm* (an upmarket farm shop with a restaurant). The food was not particularly fancy or imaginative. Just very good quality ingredients, nicely presented. As usual we chatted away about the past, present and future. However, during the meal Lou suddenly had a stricken look and burst into tears. Whatever was happening, I was not aware of it. She seemed to be staring at something that was happening right in front of her, but invisible to me. I found out later that that was exactly what was happening, she had a kind of vision.

Later she told me that, it felt as if a curtain had opened in front of her and she could see crowds of people who were clearly in distress. These people were calling to her to help them. Instinctively, she just knew that they were the families and partners of alcoholics, and they were desperate for help and support. All the time she felt that they were calling out to her, and through her to me, to somehow come and save them. Clearly she was shaken up by the incident.

When we discussed it later, we both agreed that it felt as if we were being called to help in some way. Indeed, when we looked at our skill sets, it felt that we were admirably, if not uniquely, equipped for the task. Lou's first husband had been an alcoholic, which meant that she had firsthand experience of the family side of the issue. Lou was also a trained counsellor with her own practice, so she also had the skills and experience to help people with traumas.

I had plenty of firsthand experience of alcoholism from the drinker's perspective. I was also a psychologist, an academic who studied addiction and had written and delivered the training course for addiction counsellors at Master's level. I had also carried out the world's first research project using computer assisted treatment for alcoholics. This had led to me creating one of the first online interactive self-help websites to provide alcoholics with the help they needed to recover, which had recently won a couple of awards.

At the time there was a real feeling of 'destiny', that we had not so much found each other again, but had rather been brought together for a specific purpose. Since I already had a functioning website for drinkers, it seemed natural that we should create another specifically for the families of drinkers. So we created *bottled-up.com*.

We decided to call it *Bottled Up*, as a deliberate pun. It was a riff on the bottle representing alcohol and also to signify the families' tendency to secrecy regarding their drinker and any impact on the family. At the time, and still today, there was very little help and support for the families of drinkers. The support that was around tended to consist of telling partners of drinkers to either walk (actually run) away, or to throw the drinker out of the family home. Unfortunately, this attitude in the helping services had the consequence of increasing the secrecy, as it ramped up the already high levels of shame and stigma associated with an alcoholic in the family. The other support was *Al-Anon* (the 12 Step Groups for families) which, although many have found to be extremely helpful, not everyone is comfortable with.

What services did not seem to appreciate was, most of the families of drinkers loved their drinkers and were not looking for separation or divorce. They were looking for a way to live in peace with their drinker, preferably with their drinker being abstinent. This was one of the main benefits of *Bottled Up,* that it provided an alternative to the mainstream approaches.

One of the great attractions it offers is that we provide information from both sides of the issue, Lou from the family perspective and me from the drinker's viewpoint. But more than that, this information is embedded in science and current best practice. The information is presented in a number of different ways. Text is the obvious one, where we structured the program in a simple and logical way. We also employed audio, so that people can download and listen while they walk, exercise in the gym, or drive their car.

One of the features that many of the members seeme to like are the videos. Our style is no script, no rehearsal, just take a topic, start the camera and then Lou and

I have a conversation around the topic. This medium allows us to discuss the issue from the perspectives of both the family member and the drinker. We call this a 'Heart to Heart' as we were trying to capture the informal, but intimate, feel of the member sitting having a cup of tea and a chat with us.

Another important feature of *Bottled Up* is that we try to imbue our program with our Christian values–discretely. Indeed, we made the conscious decision that the website would not be overtly Christian. Our rationale being that families of drinkers had to negotiate many hurdles to get any help and support and, the last thing we wanted was to add another one by presenting as a 'religious' program. For many people this may be off-putting, depending on their attitude towards Christianity. Later, we created another website [*beautyforashes.co* – now a self-contained section on bottled-up.com] that contained helpful videos for anyone who was looking for help of a more spiritual nature.

A friend of Lou's, who liked what we did, put us in touch with an editor from the publishing company *Lion Hudson*. We met with the editor in a coffee shop in London and told her about what we were doing and she was extremely interested. So much so that she immediately gave us an advance to write the book *Bottled Up: How to Survive Living with a Problem Drinker*. On completion of the book they then asked me to contribute to their book series called *First Steps Out*. This series was aimed mostly at providing some self-help resources for mental health issues such as anxiety and depression. They wanted me to write *First Steps Out Of Problem Drinking*. Both of these books were published in 2010 and are available on Amazon and other booksellers.

One of our goals was to partner with the addiction treatment community. So we tried to attract partners locally, especially among the treatment fraternity who were already supporting problem drinkers. This proved to be largely fruitless. Initially there was some interest, we even gave a couple of seminars where there appeared to be a real buzz about our approach. However, sadly there was no further follow up. Indeed, no one appeared to be capable of making a decision, even when we made it clear that we were offering to work with families for free. Many of the services informed us that they already had services in place to support families. However, on further investigation we later found out that these 'services' largely tended to be a paper exercise. That is, these services had been included in the paperwork describing their services when they were applying for funding. Sadly the reality was a different story.

In the years since we created *Bottled Up*, few families who have used our services have mentioned any support from their local addiction services. In fact, many of them report being excluded from any involvement in, or even any information about, the treatment their loved one is being offered. I understand that confidentiality is an issue, but it feels more of an excuse. It also seems very short-sighted, as the research suggests that having a good social network (social capital is the current term used) is helpful not only to initiate change but also for its maintenance. And the family should be seen as an integral and helpful part of that network. So excluding them from any involvement in the recovery process feels like neglecting one's best asset, especially since the major part of recovery takes place outside of the treatment rooms, in the real world.

I admit that I did struggle a bit with the lack of interest shown in our work. In Scotland I was well known in the addiction treatment field, after all I had trained many of them. Whereas now I was in Devon, I was unknown. So doors that would have previously been open to me were now, if not exactly closed, very difficult to get beyond. It was a difficult and slightly dispiriting adjustment to accept.

One of the issues that agencies seemed to have with us, was the fact that we were mostly online. At that time there was a strong belief that for any therapeutic process to be successful, there needed to be a face to face, in person meeting. I tried to explain that using the power of the internet to help and support people was not only a valid way of working, for it could also substantially reduce costs. A major issue when providing a service in Devon, a highly rural county, is that much of the population is scattered in small villages. Thus online meetings, either groups or one-to-ones, could reach this population much more efficiently and economically. The irony is that the very organisations designed to help people change are themselves too bureaucratic and difficult to change!

However, ten years later, when Covid isolated us all, they 'discovered' that they could run meetings remotely. That was a bit frustrating and made me want to scream at them, "I told you so!" Yes, I know it would have been uncharitable, but it would also have been understandable, and maybe a wee bit satisfying (forgive me, I'm a work in progress).

Over the years, *Bottled Up* has attracted members from all over the world. Naturally, our main audience lies in the English-speaking nations, but we also receive a significant percentage of our members from non-English speaking nations. Although some, but by no means all, of these are expats.

In the beginning, we charged a modest membership fee (£7 a month). As you can see, clearly this was not a 'get rich quick' scheme, nor even a 'get rich slowly' one. At the time, all we really wanted was the opportunity to help people, and cover our expenses. After a couple of years, we were approached by a marketing company who wanted to promote us by bringing in a couple of experts to build the website and market the brand. At first we were very tempted, as they were talking lots of money. If I'm honest, it seemed a really sweet proposition, helping people and getting rich too. What's not to like? However, after a couple of planning meetings, we quickly found that the control of what we would do, and even the ethos of *Bottled Up* was quickly slipping away. We knew what we wanted to provide and did not feel that such a commercial partnership would be the best way to do that. As business people they were obviously highly focussed on making money and less on the families who needed help. For that reason, we dissolved the collaboration before it really got started, and blew our chances to become millionaires. Do we regret it? Not really, but sometimes particularly when the bills come in, well...!

A year before Covid happened, we started having discussions with a large local church, that was part of a Pentecostal movement, consisting of many churches. The discussions were about how we could adapt *Bottled Up* to be a resource for these churches. Part of the plan was to bring the website for drinkers together with the families one. Then we would have a resource for both within the same website, but with different membership areas. This would be quite an undertaking, and a large financial outlay.

Also when we were praying about the website, we clearly heard The Lord say that we should make the website free for both families and drinkers to use. At the time we had hoped that the churches would contribute to the expense of the website and its upkeep. Otherwise we were not sure how we could accomplish this task. However, it seems that God had a plan. Firstly, *Internet Creations,* a Scottish based website company who built my first website, agreed to be our sponsors and build the combined website for us at a significant discount. Second, we also received an unexpected gift of £10,000 from a local pastor, which would allow us to complete the renovations on the website, and to meet all the costs for a year.

Unfortunately, Covid hit us during the changes and all the plans to partner with the churches ground to a halt. Then, by the time that Covid eventually passed, the people that we had been planning with had moved on; so, the project fell through. Regardless, we managed to combine the websites, and *Bottled Up* is now a 'one-stop-shop', having resources for both drinkers and their families. Also, we made the website free to use and were still reaching large numbers of people in the UK and worldwide.

Then there was another significant happening during this period. Prompted by the church we were planning with, we applied for and successfully acquired a grant from *Google.* Amazingly the grant was for $10,000 a month of free advertising. This brought thousands of visitors to our website, which was great to see. Unfortunately after almost a year, *Google* changed its rules in regard to their grants. The outcome was that while we technically still have the grant, the new rules prevent us from actually being able to use it. This situation has been created by a bureaucratic technicality, that is too complicated and far too boring to explain here. But it is really frustrating to have a grant which is unusable. However, we did have use of it for almost twelve months which allowed us to reach people we would never have been able to otherwise, and for that we are thankful.

Therefore, a year or so later we again needed to explore ways of sustaining the website, preferably still free to use. This time we introduced what we called the 'Chain of Care'. Basically this consists in asking anyone who has benefited from the free use of the website to contribute to its upkeep. Since, with the help of others, we had provided the website free to them, their donations in turn would be keeping it freely available for others who came later. That way they were not paying for themselves but for others. We feel it is a good Christian principle which might also foster a sense of ownership and community.

Over the years we have offered one-to-one sessions, where drinkers or families of drinkers could get to talk to us, well mostly me, as Lou had her own long established counselling practice. This was a paid service, unless they could not afford it, then we gave it for free. The majority of the clients tended to be partners or relatives of drinkers who were looking to find a way to help their drinker. We have always told them that we do not have any magic formula that will change the drinker. However, if they were to follow the program, they would be empowered and their life would change for the better.

A few months ago, someone who was helped through our website and from personal contact, offered to help us to create a series of podcasts. This was a real gift to us as he came with experience of creating content for the BBC and had directed and produced a number of programmes. As I write this, we have already recorded the episodes and just launched them. So, hopefully this will provide a new medium for us to communicate to people in need and will allow us to reach a new audience.

As a ministry *Bottled Up* has been frustrating, infuriating and, at times, even dispiriting, as people don't recognise or appreciate what we have provided.

However, overall it has also been so rewarding. Every now and then we get an email or message telling us that what we have written or recorded has given them hope; that their lives have been changed for the better. Sometimes this change has not been the way that the person hoped but would seem to be rather what they needed.

Other times, even in the midst of tragedy people have taken the time to tell us how we have helped them. At those times we feel both proud and humble, and thankful that God brought us together to help these people.

Both Lou and I suffered badly because of alcohol. After we had become a couple, she told me that she would probably never have answered my letter, if I had not talked about my difficulties with alcohol and subsequent recovery. Alcohol, then, brought us together and alcohol gave us a purpose, to help others in a similar situation. This is not an uncommon occurrence. Many charities get started by people who have suffered from some difficult issue that affected their lives. I believe this phenomenon, whereby terrible experiences are repurposed in a way that will bring benefits to others, corresponds to the 'treasures of darkness' mentioned in Isaiah 45:3. Initially, when I got sober, I wanted to get away from anything related to alcohol and addiction, but as my story shows, that was not to be. God had a use for the experiences that we had endured. When he commissioned us, we were very aware of the following verses from Isaiah (61:1-3):

> [1] The Spirit of the Lord God has taken control of me! The Lord has chosen and sent me to tell the oppressed the good news, to heal the broken-hearted, and to announce freedom for prisoners and captives. [2] This is the year when the Lord God

will show kindness to us and punish our enemies. The Lord has sent me to comfort those who mourn, especially in Jerusalem. ³ He sent me to give them flowers in place of their sorrow, olive oil in place of tears, and joyous praise in place of broken hearts.

This has been our purpose over the last 15 years, to bring clarity and hope to people who are trapped in the prison of addiction. And I thank God for the privilege of being able to help people. I also thank him for the gift of the internet, as it means that anyone, anywhere in the world can reach out and ask for help, without even having to leave their own house.

19: Leaving Scotland

Now that Lou and I had established that we loved each other and wanted to get married, there were a few details that needed to be addressed. The first, and most obvious, of these was that we lived at opposite ends of the country. Clearly, one of us needed to move. Or we could have compromised and met in the middle, around Preston, but that was impractical. When we weighed up the possibilities, we decided that the only practical solution was that I should move to Exeter. The main considerations came down to people, more precisely dependents. I did not have any dependents in Scotland. However, Lou had her teenage daughter Cassia living with her, her son in care in Exeter and a housebound, invalid mother living in Seaton. So, there was no contest. I needed to be the one to move.

The issues that I needed to deal with before we could be together were, my house and my job. As mentioned earlier, Sheila owned 20% of the house in Kilcreggan and initially she refused to give permission for it to be advertised for sale. However, eventually she relented, and I could start to remove one impediment to the move to Devon. But even after she had given permission, it was not a quick process. Kilcreggan is a lovely place, sitting on the banks of the Clyde estuary. The house, The Copse, was a magnificent Victorian mansion, originally built for a wealthy timber merchant around 1880. In the 1950s it had been divided into an upper and lower flat. I had the lower flat with the main entrance and almost an acre of garden. The outlook from house was wonderful. Being elevated meant that it had an amazing 180 degree views of the estuary, and the Isle of Arran in the distance. For me that was the real selling point. When I first viewed the house, I had fallen in love with those views, and I would sit at that window in the evening and watch the ever-changing views of the seasons.

Regardless, desirable though the house might be, there was a problem, it sat on the end of a peninsula, so it was remote. The nearest supermarket was 20 miles away and my commute to Paisley University was a 70 mile round trip. But it was such a glorious commute, through some beautiful countryside and down Loch Lomond side. I loved it, but it was definitely not for everyone. That fact, unfortunately, meant that there were few buyers, so the house took a long time to sell, and I eventually had to accept an offer below the market value.

The second issue was my job. I had worked at Paisley University for over 12 years and I had tenure (basically a job for life). There were also a few projects that I was mainly, or solely, responsible for. One of these projects was the distance learning. For a course to be relevant, it needs to be updated at regular intervals, to include and reflect advances and innovations in the field. Our distance learning materials were scheduled for an update within the next year. And, since I had written most of the original course, I would in all probability be the main author for the revised course.

At the time I was keen to retain a position with the university, at least on a part-time basis. I reasoned that, since we are talking about students being able to access tuition remotely through the internet, it did not require a great deal of imagination to see that the tutor could also access the students remotely. So, I proposed that I could remain a member of staff, even though I would be living in Devon. To me it seemed like a win-win solution. The university would not need to find a replacement, and I would rewrite and deliver the material that I had created in the first place. The Dean and Head of Department said they would consider the proposal and get back to me.

Months passed without an answer being given, I had even accepted an offer on my house. It felt like, and probably was true, that the university was stalling. I was a senior lecturer, so they could replace me with someone on a much lower salary. Also I am, and always have been, useless at departmental politics. I have always been hopeless at going along with what the bosses say, just because they say it. I have always been a bit outspoken and am not slow at pointing out a stupid idea when I see it. As I'm sure you can imagine, this could, and did, get me labelled as being difficult and, from their point of view, that was probably true. So, maybe they saw this as an opportunity to be rid of me. They could get someone cheaper and more malleable, so who could blame them.

After some more months, I asked for a meeting with the Dean and Head of Department. The only question on my agenda was had there been any progress on my proposal? Had they come to a decision yet? The answer was a lot of humming and hawing mostly consisting of

'Well you see, it's like this'. I just let them waffle on for a bit. Then I said, "Now you may not have come to a decision but I have", and I took an envelope out of my pocket and placed it on the table. "That is my resignation letter. The terms of my contract are that I have to give you one month's notice. This is that notice. Please ensure that the personnel department make all the arrangements regarding salary owed as well as my pension." Their faces showed that they were shocked. It seemed that they were expecting to string me along for a lot longer with the carrot of a possible alteration of my contract to a remote employee. But I no longer had any faith that they were going to deliver on my proposal. It felt like they lacked the imagination to see the benefits, or maybe they really did not want to have me around anymore.

My feelings were mixed about leaving the university. On the one hand I was very excited to be beginning a new life married to Lou. However, if I were to stop and think about this life change, the excitement was also tinged with a bit of fear. I would no longer have a job or a salary, or the status of a university lecturer. Also I was moving away from all my friends, the familiar aspects of my life and the countryside I loved. I was moving to England, to somewhere I did not really know, and I was moving into someone else's house. So, if I'm being completely honest, this was all a bit scary.

In some ways, I was understandably sad to be leaving my former life behind and also a bit unsure that I was actually doing the right thing. On one of those days of doubt I was driving to work. The route takes one through the lovely, almost trafficless, Glen Fruin down to Loch Lomond. At the highest point there is a wonderful view back over the Gareloch and Helensburgh. While I was driving along, I was chattering away with God, asking for reassurance that I was not making a huge mistake.

Suddenly the grey clouds parted and a shaft of sunlight like an arrow shone down towards my house in the distance. It was quite a spectacular phenomenon. After pausing to watch this light show, I found myself saying to God "I just need a sign to know that I'm right." I heard a warm voice in my head saying, "You asked for one and I've just given you one. Didn't you like it?"

"Oh, I see, so you were just showing off." I felt God smile. It is a lovely, and loving, sensation.

I felt ambivalent as I left Kilcreggan and Scotland. On the one hand I was leaving a place, a house and a country, that I loved, and I knew that I would miss the views from my front window, along with the majesty of the mountains and lochs that I lived among. However, I was also excited to be going south to be with, and to marry Lou and start a new life in Devon.

Lou lived in a four-storey Victorian house, so there was no shortage of space for me and some of my furniture. Although we did need to clear out some of the existing clutter before we could add mine. Lou's late husband, Steve, had been an antiques dealer so the house was crammed with stuffed animals and assorted knick-knacks, and the top floor had been used for storage. Once we cleared that out, I established my office up there. It was all very comfortable, my only concern was the distance to the kitchen and a cup of tea, my office being on the top floor and the kitchen in the basement. When I'm working, my fuel is tea, I grind to a halt if I am not lubricated on a regular basis. Once we established a tea station up there, I was very comfortable and very happy.

Stepfather

One aspect of my new life that I had not given much consideration to, if at all, was that Lou had two children, actually they were young adults. By marrying Lou, I was now a de-facto stepfather to Jacob (22) and Cassia (17), regardless of whether or not I wanted that role. As far as they were concerned, Jacob welcomed a new male figure in his life. His relationship with his dad had been pretty fraught. So he was glad of a new start. Cassia had different ideas. She had had a dad, and I was not it! As far as she was concerned there was no vacancy for dads in her life, thank you very much. I was welcome to be husband to Lou, and maybe even stepdad to Jacob. She was also quite happy to have me in the house, but daddy-type things, emotions, authority, etc. were most definitely off limits. I can't say that I was particularly upset by Cassia's attitude towards me. She was friendly enough which was fine by me. Anyway I was not looking to become a dad, step or otherwise. I was in Devon to marry Lou, not to acquire and or raise a family, that was definitely not part of my plan.

The house, in particular the lounge, felt a lot like a shrine. Steve's photo was looking down on me from the alcove, where all his possessions were arranged neatly. His eyes seemed to follow me round the room. Possibly I was a bit paranoid, but I'm sure that he looked at me in a very disapproving manner. Almost like he would haunt me, if I were to upset his family. In the middle of the room, with the most commanding view of the TV was Steve's old chair. It was a recliner that had most certainly seen better days. This was where Cassia sat, maybe it made her feel closer to her dad or maybe it was to guard the chair against anyone, e.g. me, who may sit in the chair and desecrate it.

When I first arrived from Scotland, Jacob was not living at the family home. He had been in care for a couple of years as he had been having difficulties at school and also within the family home. Eventually, rather late in his school life, he had been diagnosed as having severe Attention Deficit Hyperactivity Disorder (ADHD). People with ADHD have difficulties maintaining attention with any tasks, also they can have high levels of impulsivity which can lead to behaviour issues and relationship problems. Cassia also has ADHD but to a lesser degree and the more dreamy kind. The difficulties she experienced with her older brother had led to Jacob being placed in care for her safety. Jacob's overeating, which had always been an issue, then increased and he became morbidly obese. At that time, we believed that he would always require care and would never hold down a job or live independently. However, he would come to surprise us.

As I said above, I arrived in this situation without having given much thought to step-fatherhood. I assumed that since they were both young adults, my paternal input would not be welcome or required. With Cassia the former was correct but with Jacob it was different.

Coming into an existing household can be a bit difficult. The patterns of life, interactions and communications have been established, sometimes for many years, and can be resistant to change. I felt that this was particularly true in this case, that any attempt at imposing my way of life would be, at best, unwelcome. So, I adopted a softly softly approach, as clearly this was not a case where the Victorian Stepfather's Handbook was going to be helpful to me. Another plan was needed.

Much as I may like to take credit for devising the strategy that did accomplish change, and made me a full member of the household, with a say in what happened, I can't. Change came as a by-product of what happened on our honeymoon. While we were away in the South Hams in Devon, we found a brand-new lodge park that was just being created. The idea of having a bolt hole to get away was something that we both found appealing.

Lou and Steve had bought a caravan in France, in the Vendée, which we still owned, and I had previously had one in Inveraray, so we both enjoyed having a holiday home that we could take some time out whenever we felt like it. South Hams, although lovely, was a bit far away from Exeter.

Instead we found a lodge park nearer to home in Finlake, Teignbridge. It was a lovely place, around 130 acres, so plenty of space, indoor and outdoor swimming pools, gym and a quite decent restaurant. The lodge had three bedrooms, a huge open plan lounge, kitchen and dining room and a massive wrap around deck. When we bought the place the park manager tried to persuade us to also buy a hot tub. At that time I had no interest in one, but he suggested that we would be able to let the lodge much easier, and for more money, if we had one. Since the fees for the park were very expensive, we would need to let the lodge for a part of the year to make it affordable. Despite my initial scepticism, I absolutely loved the hot tub. In fact when we sold the lodge, moved house and rebuilt Lou's mum's house for ourselves, one of the first things we did was to buy another hot tub, and we still love it.

When we bought our lodge, Lou suggested that we tell Jacob and Cassia that it was mine. This did have some truth, as I bought it from the proceeds of my house in Scotland. The main reason for telling them this was in order to start living in a different way, and to give me some authority, without seeming to trample on the memory of their dad. Most of the changes were fairly small, like not having the TV on all day, and leaving it off while we ate dinner. And all sitting round the table to eat and talking to each other. The key change that we made was that Jacob had a room of his own in the lodge, and so was becoming part of the family again. A bit awkward and tenuous at first, gradually it became the norm that Jacob would be around whenever we went to Finlake. It was a subtle way of bringing him back into the family, without making it a hugely dramatic and significant gesture, which could have added pressure and tension to the process.

The other consequence of buying the lodge was that it brought changes to our way of living back home in Exeter. After some time of staying at Finlake for some short and some longer periods, Cassia decided that she would like us to turn the TV off, sit round the table and talk to each other when we ate. She discovered that she liked family time, and now accepted that I was part of it. OK, maybe she did not say it verbally, or at least not out loud, but her behaviour towards me was warmer and she seemed to appreciate that I brought something positive to the house. Over the next few years there were some very significant, surprising and touching changes in our relationship.

The first of these came when Cassia applied to university. She needed to fill in the application for a grant and some of the questions asked about the finances, income etc., of her parents. One question that caused the difficulties was, when it asked for the relationship between her and me. The obvious, and of course legally correct, answer was 'stepfather.' Prior to this we had never discussed our relationship beyond her assertion that "her father was dead and she did not want or need another." Regardless about how either of us felt or acknowledged what our relationship might be, this was a legal document. So I entered 'stepfather' in the required box. This did not go down well with Cassia, who became extremely upset and angry. Lou said that she would talk to her but I said no, I needed to be the one who dealt with this issue.

When I joined her in the living room she was sitting crying. I just sat there for a couple of minutes, saying nothing. Then when she had calmed down a little I said, "I can understand that you are upset, and you don't want a replacement for your dad. I get that. I can honestly say that I have no interest or intention of replacing him. No one can do that. But, has it ever occurred to you, that I might not actually be looking for a daughter? When I came down here, it was to marry your mother, not to adopt a family. The forms that we have just filled in are legal documents and I must complete them honestly. That does not mean that our relationship has changed in any way or will change in future. I don't want to be the new Steve, I just want to be the old John. Well maybe not old."

This little speech seemed to confuse and reassure her in equal measure. To her, I must have seemed like some occupying army come to colonise and take possession of the house, her mother and herself. Why would I want anything different? We shared a hug and she seemed to be calmer and, a bit, reassured that I was not going to plant flags on all the furniture and population of the house. But I don't think that she was totally convinced.

The next change in our relationship came a couple of years later. At the time we, Lou and I, were involved in the running of The House of Prayer in Exeter. We had some visitors from the USA who had come to speak, minister and lead worship for three days. On one of their days, Cassia had come with me. So I introduced her to the group, saying "This is Cassia, Lou's daughter." She then punched me playfully on the arm and said, "Your daughter too." I was extremely surprised. This was the first time that she had ever acknowledged me in that role. It really took me aback as I was not expecting it and was not entirely sure what I thought of it. I had gotten used to our casual relationship and was not entirely sure that 'I' wanted it to change. When I told Lou about it, she was delighted by the development.

The next event was much more emotional, and even more of a surprise. I was working in my office at the top of the house when she knocked on the door and asked, can I come in. She just sat down and it was quite obvious that she wanted to say something, but was having some difficulty with it. I just waited. You could almost taste the silence. Eventually she gathered her courage and said, "I want to tell you that I love you, but it feels like I am betraying my dad." Well, that was not what I was expecting!

Tears were rolling down her face and she was so obviously struggling with her emotions. I went over to her and hugged her then joined in with the tears. This was a huge moment for Cassia. It was not an inconsiderable one for me either. She had been very brave in declaring her feelings, and now she really needed reassurance that this act did not represent an abandonment or betrayal of her beloved dad. We just sat there hugging and crying, sharing a box of tissues. I repeated that I couldn't and would not want to replace her dad. Her memories of him would always be with her, and they were precious. I had a different place in her life and it was entirely possible to love two, three, more people. Love was not like a cake that giving a slice away meant that there was less for everyone else. It was more like a lake that never ran dry, there was plenty to go around.

That night there was a definite shift in our relationship. She had shown her love for me and it was obvious what it had cost her to do so. For me, I had gained a daughter. And I realised that I did actually want her to be my daughter. It was a hugely impacting event, probably for both of us.

Although there have been many lovely moments, the final one I want to mention represents one of the proudest moments of my life. Cassia was getting married to Scott and she was trying to decide who should walk her down the aisle. Candidates for the honour were me and Jacob. I did not want to put any pressure on her, as I strongly felt that she needed to be left to make her own decision. However, if I am honest, which I usually am, I would have been very disappointed, and even hurt, if she had chosen Jacob rather than me. Yes, I know that it is the bride's day and all that. But I would probably have smiled through gritted teeth and tears, if I did not get to be father of the bride. Fortunately, my ability to act happy in the face of disappointment was not put to the test and she selected me for the job. Thank goodness! That day, I felt so proud. My wee lassie was getting married and she looked beautiful and I got to be the one who gave her away. I felt very emotional as we entered the church. Later, during the speeches I blamed an allergy to the flowers. I'm not sure I got away with it as the flowers were artificial, to stop the real allergy sufferers having a reaction. It was a good day. Whenever I see the photos of the day, I find myself smiling and remembering what a great wedding it was and how much everyone, especially me, enjoyed themselves.

With Jacob, my memories have been less emotional but, at times, no less dramatic. My earliest memory of him happened before I had actually moved down to Exeter. We had decided to completely revamp Cassia's bedroom. So we needed to strip the old wallpaper off the walls, paint the whole room, lay a new laminate floor and build a bed, cabinets and wardrobes from Ikea. Jacob came to help with the preparation stages, stripping the wallpaper. OK, I agree that stripping wallpaper is not the most exciting task in the world. It is boring and laborious, but it just needs to be done. Jacob volunteered to help. Problem is that a boring task and a Jacob with raving ADHD are most certainly not a great mix. Every time I turned round he had disappeared down to the garden to have a cigarette and play on his phone. To say I was frustrated would be a gross understatement. I was not happy, and I just wanted him to go back to his flat. That would be easier than trying to supervise him and, supervise myself in case I should say something that would cause a rift in this fledgling relationship.

When I spoke to Lou about it, she was sympathetic to both of us. Why she should be sympathetic to Jacob was a mystery to me. Sympathetic to me, absolutely but sympathetic to Jacob, duh! She pointed out that Jacob really did want to help, his heart was in the right place. I pointed out that if he was going to help, then I needed all of him in the right place, not just his heart. Strangely my remarks didn't help.

Cassia, Lou and I hired a van and set off to Bristol to, what was at that time, the nearest *Ikea*. After what seemed like weeks, we emerged from the store with masses of furniture for Cassia's room. Jacob again volunteered to help with the construction of the furniture, to which I agreed, reluctantly, very reluctantly. I pointed him at a box, handed him some tools, and left him to get on with it. I fully expected him to disappear to the garden again, and was prepared to just accept and be thankful for when he actually did something, anything. However, surprisingly he actually showed both an interest, and an aptitude for building Ikea furniture. We were all amazed and absolutely delighted. It showed that there were hidden depths to Jacob that so far had not been discovered, it showed a lot of promise.

The next big revelation came a couple of years later. Lou and I decided that we should have a family holiday and that we should go somewhere warm. So we decided on Minorca. We rented a villa, near the sea, with a swimming pool and also hired a car so that we could tour the island. This was the first time that we had all been together for a protracted period. We had been to Finlake for a weekend, or even a week but, even then, usually Jacob did not stay to the end of the week. He just got restless and wanted to go home. Everyone was a bit on tenterhooks, as this was a full fortnight together. Two things happened on that holiday. Cassia had a mysterious new boyfriend, who she kept disappearing to phone or text. This turned out to be Scott, now her husband. And Jacob showed us a side of him that no one had really seen before. He was thoughtful and kind, and most of our worries just melted away. In fact we all had to reevaluate our feelings about Jacob afterwards, and this new impression of Jacob gave him a lot of latitude whenever he reverted to his previous behaviour.

A couple of years later, he was recommended for possible bariatric surgery to help with weight loss. It was not, however, automatic. Before they would commit to the expense of the procedure, he would need to attend a group for eight weeks. This group was to learn to eat well and to introduce a healthy lifestyle so that they could demonstrate that they could maintain a healthy lifestyle after surgery. So, all the participants needed to prove that they could actually lose some weight before they would recommend the surgery. At first we were sceptical about Jacob managing to complete the group successfully. We were also sceptical that the NHS was asking people, with a proven track record of failure, to diet to lose weight before they would give them the help they sought. That seemed counter-intuitive. Again, Jacob surprised us. He qualified for the surgery, one of the few that started in the group. And the NHS carried out the procedure.

The change over the next few months, was nothing short of miraculous. He lost 14 stone in weight and was almost unrecognisable from his previous obese self. He got a job in a supermarket, which he hated. Then he started working as a carer, which he loved. This was a job that allowed him to express his pastoral side, that he had inherited from his grandfather via his mother. He particularly liked when he was working with young and/or vulnerable adults. For it was in this arena that he showed his aptitude for enabling his clients to grow in independence. This was a joy for Lou and me to see, as through this work he also grew in independence and confidence. Over the next few years he managed to get his own flat, learned to drive and get married. The change in Jacob from the immature and troubled young man I first met, to where he is now is remarkable. It is a wonderfully inspiring story and we are immensely proud of what he has achieved.

20: You Believe What?

Moving to Exeter had a big effect on my life, obviously. I had left my country of birth, a house that I loved, a job that I had once loved but now less so; plus I had left my friends. Instead, I was living in England, back in a city, with a new family and a new career. So clearly there were major changes for me. However, almost certainly the biggest changes were internal. They were the psychological and spiritual changes.

As I discussed earlier, much of my life was trying to find a spirituality that was right for me. This was why I dabbled in various branches of eastern mysticism. Even my substance use was part of that search. Now I had found one that I thought was the answer, but I was not completely comfortable with it. I had done something that, 30 years before would have been unthinkable. I had 'turned my coat' and become a Protestant! A vision of my grandfather's funeral, and the three men dressed in black came to my mind. No one spoke to them, or even about them. Why would they? After all, they were dead to the rest of the family. And now I had joined them, and there were four men standing on the fringes.

Of course we were living in a different age. The old bigotry and fierce tribalism of my youth was no longer as strong. But it had certainly not disappeared entirely, and one of the big surprises was, that it was still there in me. If anyone had asked me, I would have said that I was above all that kind of thinking, had been for years. But I was to find that going against all that weight of early conditioning was more difficult than I could have possibly imagined.

I still carried many of the beliefs and prejudices that I had learned as a child, especially in respect of the nature of God and how we should interact with him. They may be hidden, but scrape the surface and there they are. My Greek Chorus had a whole new section all about "Turning my coat" and "What would your mother say?" If I was going to live comfortably as a Christian, and I wanted to, then I would need to be more open-minded firstly to acknowledge and then to negotiate these prejudices.

The first of these was finding a church that suited both Lou and I, which was quite difficult at the start. I was very unsure about all these different ways that Protestants communicate with God. As a Catholic you knew where you were. Mass was Mass, was Mass. It did not matter where you went, it was always the same. After the move away from the Tridentine Mass (where it was conducted in Latin) we would find that the language would change according to which country we were in. But otherwise the service would be immediately recognisable. I was to find that this is not the case with Protestant services. No these could be very different indeed.

Anyone who hangs around Christian meetings, especially charismatic meetings, will probably notice that Christians often behave oddly. There is often a lot of laughing, crying, shaking and falling over, all going on. To the uninitiated visitor it may seem a bit like visiting a mad house and they could be forgiven for thinking that. However, to the faithful this is what is known as a manifestation of the Spirit. And, yes, they do actually believe that it's a good thing!

Of course, not all meetings are like that, there are all sorts of different meetings, according to denomination and purpose. There are, of course, the stereotypical *Songs of Praise* meetings, consisting of some hymns interspersed with some prayers and a sermon. This type of service is found in most Anglican churches and various other mainline denominations.

In these types of meeting, the congregation is safely corralled in pews and tends to politely stay there and let the priest/vicar/pastor get on with it. No one expects them to do anything except stand, sit, sing and say the responses already laid out in the liturgy (the liturgy is the script for the meeting). No further participation is expected, and certainly none is encouraged! With some differences, this is the kind of religious service that I was brought up with, so it is very familiar to me.

However, in the so-called 'free' denominations, this separation of congregation and clergy can be more fuzzy. To illustrate this difference, we can use a football analogy. In the conservative congregations the crowd stay in the terraces singing encouragement to the players, who get on with doing the playing. In the 'free' congregations, the crowd can often leave the terraces and invade the pitch, run with the ball and may even score a goal. In fact, sometimes when they are really enthusiastic, they may even tackle their own side.

This spectacle becomes further confused when many of the congregation start speaking in, what seems to be, completely unintelligible languages, with everyone speaking at the same time and no one apparently listening to anyone else. This is known as 'speaking in tongues.' Usually there is a worship band at the front, whose job it is to lead the congregation in song. But even here, some member of the congregation may burst into their own song, maybe some old favourite, in which case a bit of *acapella* singing can break out. Or more confusingly, it can be something they have made up on the spot. The band then has little option but to wait till the congregation finishes, before they can return to their meticulously planned and rehearsed programme.

For someone like me, who had been brought up in the ultra-conservative Catholic church, exposure to these 'free' services seemed bizarre and unsettling. I could not stop watching the congregation to see what was going to happen next. Why was that lady lying on the floor twitching with nobody looking after her? Or why is that rather old person trying to be a ballet dancer, and with her arthritis, that really can't be good for her. Waving a flag like that is dangerous, you could have someone's eye out. I was fascinated, horrified, amused and yet incredibly attracted to doing something weird myself, but realising how strait-laced and inhibited I was. I'm a bit better now, in fact I have even been known on special occasions to throw caution completely to the wind and take my hands out of pockets in complete abandon. So, what is happening in these meetings? How do we explain this apparent chaos?

Over the years, I have come up with a number of explanations, some less charitable than others. How I reconcile it now is like this. The Lord wants to have a relationship with us, which is the most mind-blowing bit of all. If we can get our head round that fact, then the rest of it becomes easier to understand. I grew up in an ultra-conservative church where God was mostly benevolent, but distant. Going to church was a bit like going to watch the changing of the guard. I can peer through the gates of Buckingham Palace and see that the Royal Family is there. We know they are happy that we are there because they wave at the crowds. OK, it's rather imperious but it's still a wave. However, they are not wandering around the crowds asking about their family or health. In fact, there are a whole heap of people with guns that would intervene if we were to try and initiate any such conversation.

In the 'free' churches the Lord is having multiple conversations and interactions and sing-a-longs with lots of members of the congregations. He is probably dancing with the arthritic old person (is it too irreverent to imagine Jesus in a tutu). The result is a more individual experience, as opposed to communal experience. Of course, it is not a totally individualistic experience, there are communal aspects such as the singing and the sermon. But it is within the worship that the individual interactions can be observed, and experienced. In fact it can be less like community singing and more like a jam session, particularly when the Spirit moves through the meeting.

Over time I have both experienced and been a member of various churches, with varying degrees of freedom of worship. At first Lou would take me to somewhere 'safe', where there was a definite structure. She wisely did not want to throw me into the deep end of free worship too soon, in case it completely freaked me out.

The church we are in now tends to be at the freer end of the spectrum. It even has an open mic, so that anyone who has a 'word' can get up and speak. It says a lot about how far I have come in this area that I am regarded as a regular contributor at the microphone. It says even more that I almost feel comfortable contributing.

Offering Prayer

One of the big differences between my experience as a Catholic and my current life in Christianity is the attitude to prayer. As a Catholic, prayer tended to be reciting standardised prayers that we had learned as a child. I'm not sure what other Catholics expected when they recited these prayers, but if they were like me, they would not have had high expectations of having a life-changing dialogue.

I vividly remember as a child those evenings when a member of the family, or a close friend of my parents, was seriously ill, and some of my relatives would gather to visit them. The men tended to sit around with serious expressions and drink beer, or sometimes a bottle of whisky would be produced. Someone, usually one of the women, would suggest that they should pray for the person. Then they, the women, would get their rosary beads out of wherever they kept them. I always wondered what was in a woman's handbag. Well clearly, if it was a Catholic woman's bag, one essential item would be a rosary somewhere in there, usually tangled around everything else. Maybe that was a metaphor for the place of prayer in our lives.

We children could not stay in the room with the men when they were drinking. Seems it was a rule that we would understand when we grew up. Well, I have and I don't. So, we were ushered into the room with the sick person and the women. The women, sometimes led by a priest or a nun, sometimes by one of my holier aunts, would settle into the rhythm of the rosary. "Our Father who art in Heaven ..." I thought at the time that in order for God to hear these prayers they had to be said very fast, almost like a string of sounds rather than individual words or sentences.

It did make sense to me as a child, God had to be everywhere, so he wouldn't have time to sit and listen to us saying these words at a normal speed. So, if we said the prayers very fast, he could get on to the next group of rosary sayers. The other thing that puzzled me was, that it always sounded to me as if the women were saying these devotional prayers in an Irish accent, why that should happen I don't know, particularly since we were all Scottish. Maybe rather than it being reality that it is just a trick of my memory from watching too many films, like *Angela's Ashes,* about stereotypical Catholic households.

In a nutshell, as a child my view of prayers was that they were very ritualised. They were written down and we had to learn them; to the extent that we were often tested on them during Sunday school or religious education classes. What seemed to be important was that we knew the words, it did not seem to matter particularly that we knew what they actually meant, or even that we said them with any sincerity. Watching my relatives doing 'speed rosary' only reinforced this opinion. A second confusion I had about prayer was that it seemed to be used as a penance. When we would go to confession, the priest would normally finish by telling us that our penance was, for example, three Our Fathers and three Hail Mary's. So, to my childish self it gave me the impression that praying (i.e. speaking to God) was something that we did when we were being punished, it was not associated with pleasure or good things or having a relationship with Abba ('dad' in Jesus' spoken language, not the Swedish group). It was the spiritual equivalent of being forced to tell your elderly relative, whom you only saw once a year, what you did in school that day. Not something to look forward to.

I don't want to imply that my childish impressions above correspond to Catholic 'best practice' or represents how the average Catholic would view prayer. Obviously, my opinion of prayer, its purpose and how to do it, has changed quite dramatically over the years, but back then I was confused about it. The confusion was there for all to see the first time I went along to a prayer meeting as a new Christian. The leader of the prayer group said, "Let's pray for each other, can we start by praying for you John?" My reaction was why, what is wrong with me? I could not understand why anyone would want to pray for me, if I was not gravely ill or some especially bad person. Even after the group had tried to reassure me, that they were only intending to bless me, I still felt very uncomfortable with people praying over me. Indeed, when I shut my eyes I was sure that I could hear the Irish accents and the drone of the speed rosary, which disappeared when I opened one eye to check.

Receiving Prayer

Previously I've described how during my Sidmouth period I was called out for exorcism. The first time I voluntarily asked for prayer was another strange experience for me, and probably for the people who were praying for me as well. I was attending my first ever *New Wine* event (a Christian charismatic evangelical meeting). The freedom of worship was something that I was slowly becoming comfortable with, but it was taking time. I found that not having a prayer book or a liturgy to follow was a mixed blessing. It was easy to see that turning up to encounter God and selecting set passages out of a Missal or even the Bible which you then read at him was hardly an ideal way of forging a relationship. Think about it, how would you feel if someone turned up at your house and just read your own CV – or excerpts from your biography – at you and then went away without any other interaction. It would seem a bit odd would it not; what kind of a relationship would that forge?

However, the downside of not having a book with a nice script to follow meant that we had to actually talk to God. What do you say? At first, I felt like a little boy that had been forced along to visit his stern grandfather. It was fine when my parents were in the room and they chatted away merrily. But then came the dreaded moment when they said, "Tell granddad what you did today." What!!! I'm OK hiding here being invisible, thank you very much, don't single me out. I have absolutely no idea what to say. I mean what do you say to God when he knows everything anyway? What if I tell him something and he replies, "That's not what happened at all, I know because I'm omniscient". It kind of cramps your style for making a story interesting, does it not?

Some people seem to have no problems in that area. It appeared to me then, and still does today, that there are some people who can pray up a storm. They quote scriptures by the dozen and make incredible pronouncements (called prophecies). Some of them seem to go on for hours without taking a breath. I'm not in that sort of class. I can pray a little, but I'm still inhibited with public praying.

There is another bunch who also go on for hours, but don't actually seem to say anything of any consequence. This bunch makes great long speeches full of clichés and stock phrases. They seem to be in the cut and paste prayer mould. I confess that this is purely a personal opinion, and almost certainly a very uncharitable and unworthy one. However, it often seems to me that these prayers are more concerned about being heard, than actually communicating with God or the congregation. To my ear the prayers feel a bit like the free form version of the books of liturgical prayer, or the 'speed rosarians' of my childhood.

Anyway back to my asking for prayer. I can't remember now why I asked for prayer, but I know that it seemed like the thing to do at that time. I went to the back of the building and there were about three pairs of intercessors waiting for someone to come and ask. So, I selected the ones that looked to me the most sympathetic and least judgemental – after all this was my first time and I needed them to be gentle with me, which I'm happy to report they were. They listened patiently while I told them what I wanted prayer for, then they both put their hands on my shoulder and began to pray.

I had no idea what to do, so I closed my eyes and tried to look appropriately pious. In reality I felt more embarrassed than pious. What on earth was I doing here with these people? Nobody told me how I should conduct myself, should I join in, listen quietly or what? Eventually when there was a lull in the proceedings, I said "Should I pray now?" This did not appear to be the usual procedure as they looked suitably confused. However, I had started, and it was too late to go back now, so I launched into a prayer for each of them.

Contrary to my experience in Sidmouth where I felt bemused... At the end I wandered off feeling much better, and proud of myself that I had participated in the prayers. They on the other hand looked a bit taken aback. Obviously, I had not followed the usual script and had completely confused the roles of prayer and prayee. Since that time, I have had lots of prayer, some that I have asked for and some that others decided that

I needed or would benefit from. I now have no issue with someone praying for me, any more than I would have an issue with them depositing money in my bank account. On one level this is basically what they are doing, putting a deposit in my spiritual bank account. So hey, deposit away!

The House of Prayer

For some years prior to our reunion Lou had started and run a prayer group. Initially it had been a 24-hour group where people would bring sleeping bags and take it in turns to doze off for a couple of hours while the others carried on. When we met up again, they had reduced the time to just 12 hours. The group met in a local church hall, but they had ambitions to have a more permanent dedicated space for prayer.

About three years after I moved to Exeter, the group received an anonymous donation of £40,000 to create a dedicated prayer room. This money would allow the group to rent a space and adapt it to suit their purposes. After some searching, and enquiries to local Exeter churches we found a possible building which was lying empty. It was a lot bigger than we had been looking for, it had once been a church primary school, but it could certainly be adapted for our purposes. Indeed, its size opened up new possibilities that we had not considered. When we met with the management committee of the church, they were willing to consider a three-year contract. It was a great result for us while it solved a problem for them, how best to utilise a building in a prime location and save on the maintenance costs. One of the conditions of the contract was that they insisted on dealing with the trustees of this new House of Prayer (HOP), who also had to be guarantors, that is responsible for the payment of any bills or debts. Lou and I were duly elected to fill these roles. Lou because she was the driving force of the group. Me because I had been a board member of a couple of large charities in Scotland, so I brought some experience to the table. We paid the rent for the first year. The keys changed hands and we now had a large hall with two large rooms, a kitchen and some toilets. Next we needed to make it fit for our purpose. There was no shortage of volunteers to beautify the place.

Suddenly we had an army of people with paintbrushes, carpentry tools and fairy lights, lots and lots of fairy lights. It is amazing how many Christian creative people there are around. Not sure if it is one of the gifts of the Spirit or not. However, we seemed to have a lot of them, and some of them even agreed with each other what the place should look like.

A couple, then took over as leaders and coordinated the decoration and eventually this beautiful space emerged. Actually, I should say beautiful spaces as both the large rooms were beautifully decorated. The smaller of the rooms was set up as a quiet space. It had lots of the inevitable fairy lights, as well as some large sofas and bean bags where people could pray and meditate. Sometimes we would have smaller groups there, as it was a bit more cosy, and easier to heat, than the larger room. The larger room was set up as the main worship and gathering area. It also had the kitchen and a cafe area where we could sell home baking, teas and coffees, which could supplement the funds for the HOP. Sometimes we had communal meals, where everybody brought some food to eat and share. There was a real sense of community and a genuine buzz that God was moving in this place.

We invited some well-known speakers and evangelists to come and speak. Sometimes we would have events that lasted a full weekend. Others were only one evening. It was an exciting time. All the events were well attended, in fact sometimes they were packed out. People were hungry for God and he turned up in our meetings. The attendees were, quite literally, a broad church. They came from all the local churches, so all denominations and, what was great to see, all ages, were represented. There were lots of youngsters, teens, twenties and all ages. There was a real life about the place. Sadly, it came to an end, not all at once, but in increments.

Like most enterprises that implode, it was all about money. Not that anyone wanted the money for themselves, no, it was a disagreement on how to make the HOP sustainable. The leadership, including Lou and I as trustees, discussed how we could best manage the money that we had and possible strategies to add to what we had. At the time we calculated that we had enough funds to keep the HOP afloat for three years, if we did not spend any money except on essentials. Some of the leadership forwarded the suggestion that God would provide, so we should spend the money that we had. Others, including Lou and I countered, saying God had provided, so we needed to keep this money for rent and look at ways of raising money. Also, we were guarantors, so we would be liable for any shortfalls. However, we could be convinced of their position, provided they would become guarantors instead of us.

Strangely, or maybe not so strangely, this was not a solution that seemed popular and there were no takers. Despite that, they still wanted to continue with their plans which could leave a large shortfall for our three-year commitment. Since the rent was £10,000 a year, we could have been liable for somewhere between £10,000 and £20,000. Lou and I felt that we had no choice but to resign as trustees and write to our landlords telling them that we were no longer willing to act as guarantors in the circumstances. This led to a rift where we were accused of lacking faith, which seemed to me to be deeply ironic, since they were not willing to be guarantors to their own plans.

Towards the end of the second year, the leadership passed to others as some of the original members left to pursue other projects. I felt sorry for the new leadership as there was no money left in the pot for any expenses. Sadly, but not unexpectedly, the HOP closed and never re-opened.

Looking back now, I wonder if we, or I, should have done something different. I was accused of thinking with my mind, when I should have been more open to the Holy Spirit. There may be some truth in that, as I was a fairly young Christian at the time. But the fact that HOP closed earlier than planned would appear to vindicate the decisions we (i.e. Lou and I) made at that time. What I do know is that I am glad that I got to be involved in such an exciting and pioneering venture. It touched a lot of people then, and some people still talk to me about it today. I think that I can honestly say that I miss it. I miss the community and I miss the excitement of pioneering. Time passes and we managed to have some healing about the rift, but the relationships are not as close as they were once. Maybe more healing is needed.

Sin and Shame

This was not a subject that I particularly wanted to write about. Quite possibly it may not be a subject that you particularly want to read about. Nevertheless, here it is. Because of my childhood experiences with Catholicism and the White Fathers' style of preaching I have always shied clear of topics such as sin, judgment, temptation and the Devil. Living in a postmodern age, with its sliding scale of values and ethos of moral relativism, has made this fairly easy to accomplish. However, if one is going to be Christian in anything more than a token way, then sooner or later these topics need to be addressed.

As I mentioned before, I did a bit of scuba diving. Initially it was fine to let someone else take responsibility for checking the conditions and leading the dive. However, if I was ever going to grow as a diver, I needed to learn about sea conditions, currents, underwater navigation, the effect of gases on the body and safety margins, before I would need to decompress. Knowing these things made me a safer and more responsible diver and knowing about sin and the Devil helps me in my Christian life.

Knowing about something, and knowing that knowing about it helps, does not mean that it is easy to talk about, especially out loud where people might hear me. Yeah, it's less of a struggle to talk about these things among other Christians, they already believe these things, and they almost certainly think that I am just as comfortable discussing them as they are. They are wrong! As you probably remember, I grew up as an only child. However, that did not mean that I was always alone, I wasn't. My constant companions, Guilt and Shame were always there by my side, we were like the *Three Amigos*. We could have had matching t-shirts printed. In hindsight, I can now see the effect that they had on my interactions with other people and my opinion of myself. They were almost certainly major contributors to my alcoholism.

After my faith was rekindled, one of the many differences I found was that all – at least many – of these Christians were well versed in the Bible. Some of them quoting verses for just about any topic that you happened to be talking about. I could not do that. Traditionally, Catholics were not big readers of scripture. Of course we had a Bible in our house, we weren't heathens. My mother would dust it on a regular basis and keep it safe and clean in the unlikely event that we might choose to open it, for example to answer a trivial pursuit question or settle a bet.

When I did get round to opening the Bible, I found lots of bits that were comforting, some that made me angry, some that changed my thinking, some that confused me and some that opened my eyes. One of the passages in the Bible that did the last of these can be found in the Book of Genesis. It was the story of Adam and Eve. Now I have no idea what you believe about this story, whether you think that it is a factual account or that it is an allegory. No matter. I just laughed at it, that anyone could be gullible to believe such infantile nonsense.

One day I was having a quiet time. I do that now, I talk to God and it isn't even Sunday. I was reading through my Bible from the beginning and came to the Garden of Eden story. Rather than just skimming through it as usual, one phrase leaped off the page at me and I could not get it out of my head.

Seeing me as a new convert, lots of earnest believers would talk to me about the Devil. They assumed that I believed in the existence and works of 'the enemy' just like they did. When they talked about it, I would just smile or frown (depending on which was the most appropriate facial expression, just don't get them confused) and then try and change the subject to something where I was more comfortable. Talk of the Devil brought back memories of the White Fathers terrifying all of us poor kids, and I had rejected this harsh outworking of religion.

Anyway, as I read the Eden story all of a sudden, the question God asks Adam and Eve leapt out at me. "Who told you you were naked?" What a strange question – or is it? Adam and Eve had been wandering around the garden naked for who knows how long. Clothes were not only not needed, they were actually unheard of. Marks and Spencer's were yet to open a branch there as, up to this point, there was no demand for designer fig leaves. That question charts a point in time when the normal suddenly became abnormal. Not only abnormal but unacceptable and shameful.

Everyone knows the story. Eve was tempted by the serpent and she in turn persuaded Adam that it would be good to eat from this tree as they would gain knowledge and power. The knowledge that they gained brought them guilt, shame and expulsion from the garden, along with assorted other unwelcome aspects of being human.

The wording that made this question so arresting for me was *"WHO* told you you were naked?" as opposed to "Why are you naked?" Who are you listening to that has corrupted your innocence? Clearly, whatever properties the fruit of the tree imparted made Adam and Eve susceptible to this corruption, but the active ingredient was when the Devil introduced them to shame. I identified with them.

It is impossible for me to pinpoint the moment when guilt and shame entered my life, it feels like they have always been there. Whether the loss of my siblings or my failure to become a priest was the source, I don't know. Or were these life events merely the ammunition used by my accuser to corrupt my view of myself? What I do know is that they remained with me for most of my life. They did not leave when I got sober, in fact they seemed more active, especially in that first year. But even after that they had – indeed still have – their moments.

Even after I renewed my commitment to Jesus, I just did not feel that I totally fitted. I looked at all these lovely Christians and I really liked them, they were nice people. Now, I'm not saying that I was not a nice person, I certainly have had my moments. It was just that I felt that there was a restless spirit in me that wanted more, it needed expression. What that 'more' was, or how it would be expressed, I had no idea. Worse, it felt like I was a counterfeit Christian, that I was playing a part. Of course, that allowed the guilt and shame to become highly vocal. There is no way that I would say that I had managed to solve it, but I would say that I see a way forward and this improvement is due to the writings of two men.

The first of these was a complete revelation for me. Brennan Manning was a defrocked priest and an alcoholic. But the message of his books brought hope to many, I'm certainly one. He talked about Grace and God's love for us. It made me see God and me, and our relationship in a completely new light.

> "Define yourself radically as one beloved by God. This is the true self. Every other identity is illusion." Brennan Manning, *Abba's Child*

This quote cut through the noise in my head, the voice that said that I was unworthy, not sufficient, unlovable. God had sent his son to die for me, yes, other people too, but also for me. This gospel was personal! He did this because he loved me. The voices in my head telling me anything else were lies. So, "Who was telling me I was naked?"

The fact that Manning was a failed priest, like me, and an alcoholic, also like me, made his writing about the Grace and Love of God, so much more powerful for me. If God so obviously loved this man, would he not love me too? Also that even though Manning regularly relapsed into his alcoholism, and eventually died from it, God still used him in such a powerful way. That was an enormously powerful message of hope to me. It was such a beautiful example of the 'treasures of darkness'. It demonstrated the kindness of God and his power to turn tragedy into ways to save people.

The second author was John Eldredge, who I first discovered through his book *Wild at Heart*. At the time I was struggling with the feeling of being a round peg in a square hole. I did not feel comfortable with the middle-class uniformity that seemed to permeate the church. It appeared to me that there were two books that were compulsory reading to be a Christian, obviously one was the Bible and the other appeared to be *Debrett's Book of Etiquette*. Sometimes in their company I found myself wanting to scream or say something totally outrageous, just to get a reaction. Please don't get me wrong. I thought that they were lovely people, it was just that I did not feel that I was one of them. And, if I am totally honest, sometimes I felt bored rigid in their company.

Eldredge discusses masculinity in Christian men. He encourages men to rediscover their masculinity and embrace it. He encourages us to reconnect with our adventurous side, that we need a battle to fight and a beauty to rescue. When I read this book, it spoke directly to my heart. It was a message that I needed to hear. In this age when masculinity is described as 'toxic' we must have a message that says, "It's OK to be a man; in fact it is a good thing."

Both these authors helped me on a journey of healing, a journey of self-acceptance and the realisation that it is not only OK to be me, but God actually loves me as I am. There was no call upon me to force myself into a square hole to be an acceptable Christian, I am OK as I am. I can't say that I am there yet, but I can say that I am closer than I was. Both John Eldredge and Brennan Manning have helped me to see God and myself in a new and much healthier light. There is a wonderful passage in Manning's book that really helped: someone asks the father of twelve children, which is his favourite. The father says "That's easy" and one by one he extols the virtues of each of them, saying how they are his favourite. It is such a beautiful and freeing passage.

God made us all unique, with unique gifting and abilities. He loves this uniqueness. So why would we reject this uniqueness and try to be like everyone else? I pray that one day I may see myself as he sees me. Now that would be recovery!

Epilogue

As I look back on the tapestry of my life, I see threads of pain, joy, loss, and redemption woven together into a story that is uniquely mine. It has not been boring. Indeed, it is a story of transformation – a journey from brokenness to healing, from searching to finding, and from isolation to connection.

I do regret not having been a father in the traditional sense, but I am deeply grateful for the privilege of being a stepfather. Cassia and Jacob have taught me that love and family come in many forms, and their acceptance has been a gift that I cherish. Their growth and achievements have filled me with pride and reminded me that relationships, even those forged later in life, can be profoundly meaningful.

The loss of my siblings, and the grief that surrounded it, left a lasting imprint on my soul. Being excluded from that circle of mourning and sent away as a child amplified feelings of rejection that I carried for years. Yet, through faith and the healing power of love, I have come to understand that I am not alone. The revelation that I am not an only child, that I have siblings in spirit, has brought me a sense of belonging that I never thought possible.

My early interactions with women were limited to nuns and my mother, shaping my understanding of relationships in ways I only began to unravel later in life. The later relationships I have had–some fleeting, some more enduring–have taught me about love, vulnerability, and the importance of being present for those we care about.

Through all the twists and turns, one truth has emerged: life is a journey, not a destination. It is a series of moments–some painful, some joyous–that shape us into who we are meant to be. I have learned to embrace my imperfections, to see the treasures hidden in the darkness, and to trust in a God who loves me as I am. In that vein, I now see my alcoholism as both a curse and a blessing. A curse as it almost killed me and wrecked the life of someone close. A blessing because it forced me to confront my demons to grow as a person and discover that I can use that experience to help others.

But this book is not just my story; it is a testament to the resilience of the human spirit and the transformative power of grace. It is a reminder that even in our darkest moments, there is hope, and that our struggles can be repurposed to bring light to others.

As I conclude, I do so with gratitude for the people who have walked alongside me, for the lessons I have learned, and for the opportunity to share my story. My journey is far from over, but I face the future with faith, hope, and the knowledge that I am deeply loved.

Bottled-up.com

Have you been affected by problem drinking, either your own drinking or the drinking of someone close to you?

Help is only a click away. Bottled Up is the distillation of:
- Lou's experience both as the wife of an alcoholic and as a counsellor;
- John's experience as an alcoholic, counsellor and researcher.

At the Bottled Up website you can find information, a program and support.
Find it at https://www.bottled-up.com

If you would like personal support you can connect with John on a video call at: https://bottled-up.com/1-to-1/